Picture Perfect

Picture Perfect

What You Need to Feel Better About Your Body

Jill S. Zimmerman Rutledge, M.S.W., LCSW

Health Communications, Inc.
Deerfield Beach, Florida

www.hcibooks.com

The names and identifying information in this book have been changed to protect the privacy of the individuals and some details have been combined to create composite stories. This book contains general information and is not intended to be, nor should be, used as a substitute for specific professional therapeutic advice.

Library of Congress Cataloging-in-Publication Data

Rutledge, Jill Zimmerman.
    Picture perfect : what you need to feel better about your body / Jill S. Zimmerman Rutledge.
    p. cm.
    ISBN-13: 978-0-7573-0607-5 (trade paper)
    ISBN-10: 0-7573-0607-1 (trade paper)
    1. Body image in children—Juvenile literature. 2. Body image in adolescence—Juvenile literature. 3. Girls—Psychology—Juvenile literature. 4. Teenage girls—Psychology—Juvenile literature. I. Title.
    BF723.B6R88 2007
    155.5'33—dc22

                                   2007008970

Publisher: Health Communications, Inc.
               3201 S.W. 15th Street
               Deerfield Beach, FL 33442-8190

Cover design by Larissa Hise Henoch
Interior book design by Lawna Patterson Oldfield

Contents

Acknowledgments vii

Introduction: From Me to You ix

1   Mirror, Mirror on the Wall:
When You Don't See the Beauty in You 1

2   Should I Eat This? When Worries About
Food and Weight Kidnap Your Life 25

3   The Catwalk in the Halls:
When School's a Big Fashion Show.......................49

4   Can I Please Exchange My Big Stomach
and Thunder Thighs? Dealing with
Your Body Type 75

5   2 Hard 2 Be 2 Good: Dealing with
Perfectionism...99

6   Sticks and Stones: When You're
     Teased About Your Body.................................125

7   Into My Mouth, onto My Hips:
     When You're Honestly Overweight...................151

8   A Pretty Picture: I Am Already Perfectly Me....187

Afterword
     A Brand-New Frame: My Hopes for You.....................197

Resources 201

Some Inspirations for Your Own Special Statement 211

Index..221

Acknowledgments

Picture Perfect is dedicated to Dr. Vivian Meehan, president and founder of ANAD (Anorexia Nervosa and Associated Disorders), with admiration and love. And to the memory of my beloved Cocoa.

I would like to thank Susan Cohen; Talia Shalev; Michele Matrisciani, Andrea Gold, and everyone at HCI; Martha Hansen; Dan Daly; Judith Barnard; Neela Bindu; Lynn Freedman, M.Ed., R.D., L.N.; Shana Silver; Karen Pierce, M.D.; Erin Melley, PA-C; Laurie Casas, M.D.; Josie Tenore, M.D.; Robert Zimmerman; Jane H. Zimmerman; Andrew Rutledge; Daniel Rutledge; Jonathan Rutledge; and Robert Rutledge.

Introduction: From Me to You

Dear Reader,

Did you pick up this book and wonder if it's for you? If you agree with any of the following statements, you'll probably find *Picture Perfect* helpful.

1. I feel pretty good about myself, except I'm not happy with how I look.

2. Kids at school tease me for being too fat (or too thin); I want to learn how to ignore them and feel better about myself as a person.

3. I think I might have an eating disorder.

4. My friends and family tell me I look fine. But I feel as though they're just trying to be nice, and the truth is that I'm ugly.

5. I'm a perfectionist about how I look.

6 I hate some parts of my body, for example: my stomach, my thighs, my butt, my face, my chest, my arms.

7 I can't stand it when I feel bloated after I eat or around my period.

8 I want to feel better about my body.

Girls' problems with body image, or how we think and feel about our bodies, are getting a lot of attention from researchers these days. In the past few years, several studies have shown that most teenage girls don't have a great body image. But recent findings tell us that it's not just teens who worry about their bodies—80 percent of ten-year-old girls say they're afraid of being fat, and most of those girls feel better about themselves when they are dieting. Even girls in first grade have reported that they wish they were thinner!

I wrote this book to help teen and preteen girls with the hard issue of body image. As I was planning it, I thought how helpful it would be for a girl to have some good coping skills—so she could feel better about her body instead of feeling unhappy about it. So she could accept her body type, just as she accepts the color of her eyes or her birthday. So she could feel like her body is only *one part* of the beautiful person she is.

I chose my title, *Picture Perfect,* because it means two

things. First, it addresses the fact that our culture tells girls they must be "picture perfect"—perfectly thin, perfectly groomed, have perfect hair, perfect skin, perfect teeth, perfect grades, perfect friends—to be considered successful. Since *no one* is actually perfect, this message often spells *disaster* for a girl's body image.

But "picture perfect" also means that we can *picture ourselves,* flaws and all, as, well, *perfect.* That's because no two people are exactly alike, so only you can be perfectly *you.* In that sense, you are valuable and attractive, and if you try to be someone else, you take away from being perfectly *you.* We can try to be healthier, kinder, smarter, more creative, and so on. But if we don't appreciate our specialness and uniqueness, we can't really achieve the goal of being the best—including the most attractive—we can be.

In each chapter of *Picture Perfect* I explain a major problem that stresses girls out about body image. Then three girls tell you how they've learned to deal with the problem. (I've used true-life stories I've heard from girls in my practice over the years, but the names and identifying information have all been changed and rearranged to protect their privacy.)

I invite you to talk to yourself in *Picture Perfect.* I encourage you to give yourself positive messages that I call "Special Statements." In my very favorite story, *The Wizard of Oz,*

Dorothy had a Special Statement that helped her deal with the bewilderment of Oz. Dorothy's Special Statement allowed her to feel grounded when her world was spinning out of control. It calmed her feelings, so she could envision—and wake up in—her safe, secure life in Kansas. Dorothy's Special Statement was "There's no place like home." Of course, we all need to find special, positive words to say to ourselves when we feel upset and confused, and this is especially true when we feel bad about our bodies. Every girl needs a Special Statement to boost her body image!

All the girls in *Picture Perfect* have their own Special Statements, which they share with you. The girls' Special Statements are words they say to themselves to think more positive thoughts, to *ground themselves,* and to stop feeling so bad about their bodies. Their Special Statements counteract their negative body-image thoughts and feelings by giving them benevolent, productive body-image messages to hold in their minds.

A Special Statement of your own can help you to stop putting your body down, too, and help you envision a better body-image picture of yourself. Many of the girls in *Picture Perfect* take their Special Statements to a deeper level by creating new habits and activities that support the positive messages—which they share with you.

So try out the girls' Special Statements—have fun experimenting with them. Some may work for you—say them over and over to yourself! Some may not, and that's okay—maybe you know a friend for whom they can work instead. Share them with her! Make up your own Special Statements. That's the best way—to find your own Special Statements that make you feel special and good about yourself!

Think about this: When you frame a picture, you have lots of decisions to make. You have to decide whether or not a particular frame's shape or size or color brings out the best in your picture. You have to think about the picture's composition and perspective, and whether to display it in a horizontal or vertical frame. You have to choose where to display your picture: do you want to see it every day when you wake up, or do you want to put it in a special drawer and take it out on a whim? And when you grow tired of the same old thing, you can simply change the frame. Presto! You have a new picture.

Like framing a picture, you also put your thoughts and feelings about your body in a certain framework. If your frame is drab and negative, you'll see yourself as too fat or too thin or too tall or too short—never quite right. And when you see *that* picture 24/7, you automatically feel bad about your body.

But you can *reframe* your thoughts and feelings about your body. Instead of seeing it surrounded by negativity, you can put the picture of yourself in a brighter, more self-accepting frame. And when you look at your body in this positive frame, you get a glimpse of yourself as beautiful and *picture perfect* just the way you are.

As always, I'd love for you to contact me with your questions, comments, and suggestions.

Love,

Jill

www.jillzimmermanrutledge.com

Snail mail address: 636 Church Street, Suite 404

Evanston, IL 60201

1

Mirror, Mirror on the Wall:

When You Don't See the Beauty in You

"My friends say I'm thin, but I think my thighs and hips are huge."

"My mom says I'm pretty, but she's just my mom."

"I wish I could lose five pounds."

"I wish I could gain ten pounds."

"I stayed home instead of going out with my friends because I thought I looked fat."

"All the girls in my class are cute—except me."

"I had a pimple and spent an hour and a half trying to cover it up, but I couldn't, so I stayed home from school."

Do any of these statements sound familiar?

Sometimes we don't see ourselves as other people see us. You may feel fat, even though the "mirrors" around you— your friends and family—insist that you're not. You may hate a particular part of your body, even though it looks fine to everyone else. You may see a huge, ugly flaw in yourself that no one else even notices. These feelings are called body-image distortions, and many girls feel them from time to time. Take this short quiz and see if you do, too.

Body-Image Distortion Quiz

1. I want to like my body, but for some reason I hate everything about it.

   ❏ **TRUE**   ❏ **FALSE**

2. I think a certain part of my body (stomach, legs, butt, skin, hair, ears, and so on) is very unattractive.

   ❏ **TRUE**   ❏ **FALSE**

3. I can't think of anything positive about my appearance.

   ❏ **TRUE**   ❏ **FALSE**

4. I think I'm too fat (or too thin), even though my doctor says I'm healthy and/or my friends say I look good.

   ❏ **TRUE**   ❏ **FALSE**

5. Sometimes I stay home from school because I'm unhappy with how I look.

   ❏ **TRUE**   ❏ **FALSE**

6. I often compare myself to other girls and feel inferior.

   ❏ **TRUE**   ❏ **FALSE**

7. I think everyone is more attractive than I am.

   ❏ **TRUE**   ❏ **FALSE**

Did you answer True to any of these statements? If so, you might not see the real Beauty in You.

And there can be lots of reasons for this. Here are a few:

1 You may *want* to feel good about your body, but it's such a *habit* to see yourself in a negative light.

2 You may not want other people to think you're "full of yourself," so you automatically put yourself down to appear "modest." As a result, this becomes your pattern: never to allow yourself to feel good about how you look.

3 You may feel *guilty* if you don't like your body because you think about kids in war zones who have missing legs and arms. But you still can't stop feeling dissatisfied with your own healthy body.

4 You may compare yourself with other girls who you think are "perfect looking" and become painfully aware of all your "imperfections." You may even compare yourself with models and actresses, even though you've heard that their pictures are airbrushed and computer enhanced—in short, *not real.*

5 You may have sad and/or insecure feelings about yourself in general, and they may make you feel sad and/or insecure about your body, no matter what anyone else says.

Many times a girl's negative thoughts about her body are *illogical* and *irrational.* She may think she's ugly, yet how could this be logical if everyone else thinks she's attractive? She may think a certain body part is disgusting, but this is unlikely to be true. She may think she has absolutely no good points, yet the reality is that *everyone* has at least one pleasing physical feature!

Some studies indicate that girls who obsess about their personal body flaws may also be depressed and/or anxious about other issues as well.

For example, a girl may be depressed because a boy she likes doesn't like her in the same way, and she may think, "If only I was thinner, had bigger breasts, wasn't so tall, wasn't so short, and so on, he would like me." She may focus all her negative thinking and bad feelings on her *appearance;* pretty soon, she may decide that something is wrong or ugly about her body, even though this is not a realistic, logical thought. She may also develop behaviors to deal with her negative body image, for example, wearing only black to "camouflage her fat," or constantly asking her mom or her friends, "Do I look okay?" or avoiding social situations where people might notice the "gross" feature that, in reality, only *she* sees.

If you physically matured earlier than most of your friends, you may be more susceptible to feeling self-conscious or anxious about your body, and this can interfere with your body image.

Lots of girls really like having "womanly curves." But some girls feel uncomfortable about them and the attention they may bring from other kids and even adults. An early developer may feel awkward about the parts of her body—breasts, hips, thighs, stomach, butt—that make her look "womanly." She may get compliments about her developing figure, but she may secretly feel ugly because her body makes her look different from her friends. Her body may be more "grown-up" than she can handle—she may long for the days when she was flat-chested and uncurvy.

This much is certainly clear: In our culture, it's rare to meet a girl who is totally happy when she looks at herself in the mirror. But that doesn't mean *all* girls have poor body image.

Some girls can tolerate or ignore their negative body-image feelings because they've learned to accentuate their positives. For example, if a girl doesn't like her nose but thinks her eyes are okay, she might cut bangs to highlight her eyes, or wear a little eye makeup. *Focusing on the positives* is a valuable skill: it helps you see that you were born with *something* you consider attractive, even though you may not think you're flawless. The good news is that all girls can learn to do this. Every girl can learn to appreciate and enhance her good points—which can help soften her bad body-image feelings.

Feeling unhappy and discouraged about your appearance fogs up a picture of good body image, but you *can* learn to wipe off the glass. You *can* clear off a gloomy outlook and instead gaze at your personal portrait of *body acceptance*. It may not feel natural at first, but with practice, you *can* learn to see the Beauty in You.

Here is how three girls found ways to see their own beauty. None of them had an easy time learning to accept her body, but each is making good progress. See what helps them. See if some of their ideas help you, too!

⭐ Special Statement:

"One step at a time—I like my nails."

–Cari, age 15

Cari has twin sisters, two years older. One sister wants to be a model. The other plays softball and couldn't care less about her appearance, at least for now. Cari feels jealous of the sister who wants to be a model because she's naturally very tall and thin. She gets along better with her other sister, Katie. They play sports together and many times stay up all night talking.

"Pretty" is not a word Cari would use to describe herself. She has a hard time feeling as if she's even acceptable looking. She started feeling this way at the end of eighth grade. In retrospect, Cari thinks she was anxious about leaving her middle school friends and going to a private high school. She was especially worried that she wouldn't find a new group to hang out with.

On her first day of high school, a mean girl told Cari that she had a nose like a witch. It was during lunch and everyone at her table laughed. Ever since, Cari has felt that she is a *totally* unattractive person.

"I always feel like I'm fat when I compare myself to my skinny sister. She doesn't try to be thin, but she just is—tall and thin. I'm not like her at all, and I never have been. I'm sort of used to it by now.

"But now I look in the mirror, and all I see are my defects. I'm so insecure. It's all because of what that girl said. When she said I had a witch's nose right in front of everybody, well that was it—I felt like crying. A kid who sat next to me said the girl is just mean and that I shouldn't worry about her. He even called her the "B" word. But I felt so ugly. I felt deformed. I never felt more insecure in my life. A girl told me that one of her guy friends who's in my math class told her he thinks I'm cute. But I thought she was just saying that to make me feel better."

Cari talked to her sister Katie about her feelings. This helped her feel a lot better—and also helped her find a Special Statement! Cari had always thought Katie felt okay about how she looked, but she was surprised to learn that this was not true.

"Katie said that sometimes she compares herself with our other sister, her twin, Kim, and then she feels really ugly. But she said she tries not to think about it. She tries to think of the things she likes about herself. She said she likes her arms and her eyes. So I thought maybe if I could think of a good thing about myself, it would help me, too, and maybe it would give me something else to think about when I feel bad."

Cari tried very hard to think of one thing she thought was acceptable about her appearance. She thought about her whole body, head to toe, and she decided that there's only one thing she feels okay about: her long, strong fingernails.

"My mom used to paint my nails when I was little. I've always taken care of my nails, and they grow pretty fast. I file them and put polish on, and they look all right—people tell me I have good nails. So I decided to use *One step at a time—I like my nails* for my Special Statement because it's true; I do sort of like my nails. It was hard to think of something. Liking my nails is my first step, and it's a big step for me.

"When I give myself a manicure, I feel better. I paint my nails when I feel like nothing is pretty about my body, and then I think to myself, *Well, at least one thing is pretty.* I'm hoping that I can like other parts of my body, too. I'm a long way from that now, but maybe if I go one step at a time, I'll eventually start to think I look okay. I don't think I'll ever be totally happy about the way I look, but I think I've made a little improvement. Katie said I'm right, my nails are really great, and that makes me feel better, too."

Cari put her Special Statement into action with a *special treatment!*

Action Plan

A "Mani-Pedi" Sweet Treat

Cari's birthday is in February, which can be a cold, dreary month in the Midwest, where she lives. So she decided to do something very fun and extraordinary to brighten up her big day! For her fifteenth birthday, Cari asked her mom for a special gift—a manicure and pedicure at a local day spa. She thought this would be a great treat and would make her feel attractive—and she was right!

"This was really good for my body image because my nails are my good point, and the manicurist kept telling me how lucky I am to have such beautiful, healthy nails. They don't crack or split or anything. So that was good, and it made me feel a little special, and it kind of reinforced my Special Statement. I kept thinking to myself, *One step at a time—I like my nails.* And the pedicure was amazing—I never had one before. I soaked my feet in a whirlpool bath, and the lady gave me a foot massage! She even rubbed sugar on my feet to make them smooth! My toes looked so pretty, and my feet were glowing! Maybe someday that will be the second thing I like about my body—my feet! I want to get another 'mani-pedi' at the spa in a few months and I will, even if I have to save my allowance for weeks!"

Special Statement:

"Fat is not a true emotion."

–Julie, age 16

J ulie is a good student. She has taken gymnastics since she was in kindergarten and is on the gymnastics team at her high school. Julie is the oldest of three children. When Julie was in ninth grade she had bulimia. She doesn't binge and purge anymore—now she has generally healthy eating habits. But the one thing that is left over from her eating disorder is a distorted body image: Julie thinks she's fat, even though, realistically, she's at a normal, healthy weight.

"I don't know why, but I just think I'm too heavy, even though *everyone*—my friends, my parents, my brother and sister, my doctor—says I look really healthy and good. When I had bulimia I looked sick. My body was not healthy. I never want to be like that again. I felt so tired and nervous all the time.

"But I wish I could be healthy *and* not feel fat. I've gained weight and gone up two sizes, and I don't like that—even though I know I was way too thin before. But being a bigger size makes me feel fat, even though intellectually I know I'm not. I think I've gained weight in my stomach. I think my stomach is huge, even though my mom says that girls are supposed to have stomachs that are a little rounded or we'd look like guys! But I want a flat stomach, anyway."

With her best friend, Lisa, Julie tried to explore why she felt so fat. Lisa was by her side during her battle with the eating disorder—she's the one who encouraged Julie to tell her parents about her bulimia, so they'd get her help. But even though they talked and talked, they couldn't figure out why Julie still felt so bad about her body. She hadn't binged or purged for over a year, and it didn't make any sense to either of them. Julie felt disheartened—she was afraid that she was so used to feeling fat that she would always feel that way, no matter what.

But one night at her weekly eating disorders support group, Julie found an answer to her "feeling fat" dilemma—and she also found her Special Statement.

A group member started to talk about being honest with herself and looking inside herself to find her true emotions. The group leader explained that true emotions are the feelings we hold inside that may be hard to take a look at, such as feeling out of control, feeling sad, feeling tense, anxious, or angry. Then the leader said, "Fat is not a true emotion." Another girl said she thought it was easier to say she "feels fat" than to figure out her true emotions and try to deal with them. This discussion went on for an hour. And it left a big impression on Julie.

"I still go to my support group because it helps me feel like I'm not alone in trying to recover from bulimia. Even though I don't binge and purge, I still get urges—fewer now than before, but I still do get them. And I still feel so fat.

"When that girl talked about her true emotions, I could really relate to that. It just kind of clicked for me. I decided to use *Fat is not a true emotion* for my Special Statement. I realized I was spending a lot of time feeling fat, but I was probably covering up some other feelings. That kind of helped me see my 'fat feelings' differently.

"I think *Fat is not a true emotion* is a good Special Statement for me. It's like a slogan I say over and over to myself. It does help me feel better, because it makes my fat feelings less powerful. It reminds me that when I feel fat, there must be other feelings in me, too. So when I can't stop thinking about my fat stomach, I ask myself: Am I angry? Am I scared? Am I sad? And even, am I happy? Sometimes I feel insecure when I feel happy, like that feeling is a mistake, or it won't last.

"Sometimes I can't always figure out my true emotions, but at least I try. When I figure them out, I can think about what to do about them. It doesn't always make my 'fat feelings' go away, but I realize if I don't try to dig deeper for my true emotions, there's really nothing I can do to cope with them, and I just feel fat and bad.

"Sometimes I write my true emotions down in a journal at night before I go to bed. That definitely helps me sort them out. Sometimes I talk about them in my group or with my therapist. They're so personal. My group leader says true emotions are very special and precious. In a way I guess that's true."

Here's a way Julie puts her Special Statement into action.

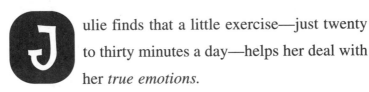

Action Plan

A Spoonful of Exercise

Julie finds that a little exercise—just twenty to thirty minutes a day—helps her deal with her *true emotions.*

"One of my friends is depressed, and her therapist told her that a little exercise is good medicine. So I thought I'd take a little of that medicine and tried exercising to help my 'fat feelings.' I have to make sure I don't get obsessive about it because I know that can lead to getting an eating disorder again. But I just exercise for a limited amount of time, so I think I'll be okay with that. My doctor said that moderate exercise is fine, as long as I don't skip meals and don't start losing weight.

"If I jog for a mile or two, or even walk for maybe twenty minutes, it really relaxes my brain. That helps because sometimes I think when I feel fat, it's because I'm totally stressed out. My true emotions are wound up inside—I really feel tense and worried. Once I was worried about something a friend said to me. She said a boy I liked asked another girl out, and this sounds so lame, but I thought it was because of my fat stomach. But then I went jogging around the block, and my mind was able to chill. I felt better, and I didn't worry so much about my stomach. Jogging helps me put all that stuff out of my mind for a while. I like to jog with a friend because it's more fun, but if I don't have anyone to go with I just go myself. Feeling better and more relaxed is worth it. And when I jog, I remind myself that *Fat is not a true emotion.* It helps me stay focused. I remember that jogging helps me deal with feeling tense and worried about lots of things besides my body—and those *are* true emotions."

Annie just started ninth grade. She thinks she has the worst acne of all her friends. Sometimes she doesn't even want to go to school because her makeup won't hide her pimples to her satisfaction. This creates a lot of stress between Annie and her mom.

"We fight all the time about my acne. I want to take antibiotics for it, but my doctor said we should wait a few months, so my parents won't let me. This makes me so mad. It stresses me out. My friend doesn't even have bad acne, and she takes antibiotics. Acne sucks. It makes me feel so ugly."

Annie's doctor did prescribe some topical acne medication that she puts on her face in the morning and at night. At first this didn't help because Annie was using too much of it—it was drying her face out, which made her acne worse. But when she followed her doctor's instructions and used less, she began to slowly see some results.

"But I still got zits. I still wasn't happy because the medication was taking too long to work. I want results immediately, right now!

"I don't like gym class, especially swimming. I'm more self-conscious about my face, but I don't want anyone to see my back, either. I have acne there, too. I always wear a T-shirt at the beach. But I'm too embarrassed to swim at the pool with my friends in the summer. My acne interferes a lot with my life."

Annie felt so bad about her acne that she couldn't see her positive parts: she loves writing stories and even got one published in the student newspaper; she is the friend that everyone comes to with their problems because she's a good listener and makes them feel better; she plays the flute. In her head, she made her acne problem *big,* and all the other positive things about herself small, as though they didn't really matter. Her mom told her that no one has a perfect life, and everyone has something they wish was different, but that didn't help Annie feel better.

Then something her mom said *did* make Annie feel better. One day when they were making the beds together, her mom told her about when she was a girl she'd go to the candy story every day after school with her friend and get a box of Cracker Jack. Annie hadn't heard of Cracker Jack so her mom explained: it was a box of caramel-coated popcorn, and inside every box was a prize.

"Then Mom said, 'That's like life. Everyone gets a prize!' For some reason, I liked that saying. It made me think about things. My mom and I talked about it for a while. She said when she was in high school she was friends with a girl who wasn't very pretty, but she had a great personality. That was her prize, and it made her attractive—everyone wanted to be around her, and everyone liked her. I think I have a pretty good personality, too. I liked the prize idea so much that I made *Everyone gets a prize* my Special Statement.

"To be honest, my Special Statement doesn't really help me feel better about my acne. I'm still embarrassed about it, and I want to take the antibiotics. I know I will someday, but I have to wait until my doctor lets me and my parents say it's okay.

"But my Special Statement does make me think about the positives. I get along okay with my family, I have five really close friends, I'm pretty smart, and when I try I get good grades. And I have a good personality. Those are my prizes. Then I thought about a girl in my humanities class who has good skin, but she's mean and no one likes her. Some people hate her. It's kind of sad, but that actually makes me feel a little better about myself. At least I have friends and no one hates me that I know of.

"When I think about my acne, which is most of the time, I try to remember to say *Everyone gets a prize* to myself, so I can think about the good things—like the people who care about me. The thing is, no one but me seems to care about my acne, and my friends don't even think it's that bad."

Here's a way that Annie puts her Special Statement into action.

Action Plan

A Fun, Fabulous Facial

Annie lives near a salon that offers acne facials for teens. She asked her mom if she could try one. Her mom was skeptical—she was afraid that Annie's acne would get worse—but she checked it out with the dermatologist, who said that it would be fine as long as these conditions were met:

1. Annie didn't have any active outbreaks.

2. It was a very gentle facial.

3. The facial technician was experienced in treating teens with acne.

So Annie tried it—and she liked it!

"I felt amazing! The facial technician was very nice, and she said she'd seen girls with worse acne than mine. It was very relaxing, and my face didn't get red or anything, and I think my skin looks a little better. I think it helped my body image, and I hope I can do it again!

Getting the Picture

Beauty can be merely physical, but the best beauty is much more than that. The best beauty is solid. It's lasting. It's feeling as though there are positives to your appearance—and your life!—that can be underlined and remembered in your mind. It's being able to see that *no one* has *no flaws*—not even the people we deem flawless!—and that our flaws don't make us ugly: it's our *attitudes* about our flaws that create feelings of unattractiveness.

Cari, Julie, and Annie all struggled with feeling unattractive, in spite of the reality that they were *all* attractive and special in their own ways. Cari felt bad about her nose and her whole physical appearance because of a mean girl's rude comment, even though her friends told her not to worry; Julie felt fat, especially in her stomach, even though everyone else told her she looked great; Annie was obsessed with her acne, even though other people, including her dermatologist, didn't think it was such a huge problem.

And each girl found a way to feel a little more beautiful about herself.

Cari tries to focus on the one thing she likes about her appearance—her nails. This helps her feel more secure so that she can see a glimmer of her own personal beauty. And every time she says to herself, *One step at a time—I like my nails,* she's building on that feeling. Sometimes she gives herself a special "mani-pedi" treat, and she's working on liking her toes now, too! Cari hopes that someday she'll be able to feel more attractive. And by slowly accepting some *positives* about herself, she'll most likely be able to do just that!

Julie uses her support group to help her think less about her "fat stomach" and more about her deeper feelings. She reminds herself that *Fat is not a true emotion,* and this motivates her to take a deeper look at herself when she "feels fat." As she shares and listens to others in her group, Julie gets a lot of insight into her own true emotions. She also finds that journaling and moderate exercise help her to deal with her feelings and feel better about her body.

Annie is slowly able to see that flawless skin isn't the only prize in life, and that she has plenty of good things in hers. She is learning to see that *Everyone gets a prize!* Even though she still feels bad about her complexion, she's able to see her acne in a better perspective, and she's beginning to believe that her life does have some positives, not just problems. She sometimes gives herself a prize—a facial! And it makes her feel amazing!

Each girl developed a Special Statement to help her remember that she possesses her own beauty, inside and out. And you can, too!

Here are six questions that can help you think of a Special Statement. Try to answer the questions rationally and honestly. Your answers will help you challenge your negative thoughts. They'll help you think of a positive message to give to yourself about your body. They'll point you in the direction of your own Special Statement.

1 If everyone else says I look fine, or even attractive, could they *all* be wrong?

2 Can any of my "imperfections" also be seen as "unique" or "distinguished" or "special"?

3 What feature(s) do I like about myself? (We all have at least one!)

4 What are the special qualities that make me a little different, in a good way?

5 What prizes do I have in my life?

6 What are my true emotions? Anger? Sadness? Fear? Happiness? (True emotions are personal and priceless. Even if they're difficult, they're all part of your inner beauty.)

So create a Special Statement!

Let it help you put your "flaws" into perspective!

Let it help you start to see that there is *real* Beauty in You.

Should I Eat This?

When Worries About Food and Weight Kidnap Your Life

Thinking about food and weight can start out to be a *good* thing. You may want to eat healthier, so you cut down on junk food. Or you may want your jeans to fit better, so you think losing a few pounds might help. Or you may know a girl who's a vegetarian, so you want to try this for yourself.

But sometimes a good thing can go overboard. That's what happens when you think about food and weight more than you think about anything else. When a good thing goes overboard, your nonstop thoughts about food and weight can take over your life. Fun can disappear very quickly! Good feelings and self-esteem can get lost. Worry consumes you. And, of course, your body image suffers. In fact, your body image may really suffer a lot.

In our culture, it is *hard to avoid* being preoccupied with food and weight. We're bombarded with messages that remind us to think about the food we eat and how many pounds we weigh. Thousands of words and images virtually cement worries about food and weight into our brains! Test your own feelings about food and weight with the following quiz.

A Food and Weight Quiz

1. I have "good foods" and "bad foods."

   ❑ TRUE   ❑ FALSE

2. I weigh myself every day.

   ❑ TRUE   ❑ FALSE

3. I try to avoid desserts because I'm on a diet.

   ❑ TRUE   ❑ FALSE

4. I feel nervous or anxious when I eat unfamiliar food.

   ❑ TRUE   ❑ FALSE

5. I feel as though I gain weight immediately after I eat a treat such as a cookie or a piece of cake.

   ❑ TRUE   ❑ FALSE

6. At bedtime I think about—and judge—everything I ate during the day.

   ❑ TRUE   ❑ FALSE

If you answered True to any of the above questions, you may also answer True to this statement:

I worry too much about food and weight.

Here are some common experiences stuck in the minds of many girls:

1 You read in a magazine that a particular celebrity is a certain size, and immediately think *you're huge* because your body is bigger than hers.

2 You read a newspaper article or headline such as "Epidemic of Obesity in Children" and ask yourself, "Am I obese?"

3 You hear people—maybe your mom or dad or a friend—talk about "low-carb" or "low-fat" diets, and ask yourself, "Is this stuff bad for you? Should I not eat carbs or fat?"

4 Your mom looks at herself in the mirror and says out loud (maybe even to you directly), "My butt (or thighs, or stomach, and so on) is too big. I need to lose some weight," and you worry that your butt is too big, and you decide you need to lose weight, too.

Of course, there's a big downside when a girl is preoccupied with food and her weight. Everyday, *normal* events (such as going out with friends or getting dressed in the morning) turn into *dramatic* decisions. You may worry too much about these things—things that you never even used to think twice about. You may ask yourself new, nervous questions, such as "Should I eat candy at the movie?" or "I love this skirt, but does it make me look fat?" or even "Should I eat a piece of my own birthday cake?"

Like a thief in the night, worries about food and weight can steal your positive, self-accepting thoughts and feelings. Worries may take up so much brainpower that you don't think of the *good things* about yourself, and the good things in your life.

So if you worry too much about food and weight, how do you stop? It's a hard question. The girls in this chapter will share their Special Statements with you and give you some of their tried-and-true solutions. They'll show you the ways they've found to stop—or at least slow down—their worries about food and weight.

See for yourself. Try the girls' creative ideas and Special Statements. See if they help *you* calm down *your own* worries about food and weight. See if they help you clear your mind, so it won't be cluttered with worries about the numbers on a scale, your jeans size, or fat grams and carbs. See if they help you have more time and energy for the *fun things* in your life.

Read on! Find something that works for you, too!

"I deserve dessert!"

—Jess, age 16

J ess is the youngest of three sisters. Her two sisters are already in college. She misses them, but when the middle sister left for school last year, Jess was happy that she inherited her big bedroom. Jess does pretty well in school and says her friends consider her "cute, not beautiful."

Jess felt okay about her body until last year, at the beginning of ninth grade. She was shocked when she was weighed for her school physical—she'd gained sixteen pounds over the summer. Her mom said, "You're fine. Don't worry about it." Her doctor said her weight was just right for her height and reminded her that she had grown a lot since her last physical. But Jess thought she was fat and wanted to lose at least ten pounds—the sooner the better. That's all she could think about.

"I freaked out when I realized how much weight I gained. It didn't matter that I'd grown three inches and everyone said I'm normal. I just really wanted to lose weight. I thought, *Oh no! I can't even fit into my jeans anymore, and they cost me four weekends of babysitting.*

"I decided I was going to give up sweets. It didn't work. My mom loves to bake, and every Saturday she makes fresh banana bread or pumpkin bread or cookies—things like that. I didn't eat any sweets for a few days. Then I had no willpower, so I ate too many sweets over the weekend. Then I got scared that I had eaten all the wrong things. It made me more worried about my weight."

One day Jess picked up a magazine that one of her sisters had left in her room. She noticed an article on healthy eating. She read the whole thing—and was very surprised at one of the tips she learned!

"I read an article written by a nutritionist in my sister's *InStyle* magazine. She said that you should eat dessert! I couldn't believe it! But she said people eat healthier during the day if they know they can have a dessert. Somehow that made it more okay with me—I could have a dessert because the magazine said it was okay. I think this made me feel less afraid of sweets because the article said that the nutritionist helps celebrities. I thought that if they listen to her, I could, too."

Jess tried out her new idea about desserts one Saturday afternoon. She also found her Special Statement at the same time.

Jess's mom had just baked chocolate chip cookies, and they smelled *really* good. Jess wanted a hot one so badly! She fought with herself—she felt if she ate one, she'd feel guilty. But then she remembered the article in the magazine. She knew that if she didn't allow herself a dessert, she'd think about the cookies all day and probably eat them anyway—in fact, she'd probably eat too many of them. That was what she usually did when she denied herself something she really wanted.

"So I decided this: I could have a couple of my mom's cookies because it's my right as her daughter. It's my right as a human being. I was so sick of worrying about eating her cookies. I thought, *My mom is a great baker. The magazine says you can have a dessert. So I'm allowed to have her cookies if I want some! I deserve dessert!* I decided that would be my Special Statement because it made me feel like I was trying to be normal."

Jess ate a few of her mom's cookies. She felt a little uncomfortable and scared, but the feelings went away. And she really enjoyed those cookies!

"I was proud of myself. I didn't go back and binge on them. I felt happy that I could have just a few and be okay with that. I had a glass of milk, too, just like I used to before I got so freaked out about my weight. I felt like I was eating like a normal person for the first time in a long time.

"I'm still struggling with accepting my weight, even though everyone says there's nothing wrong with me, and I look good.

But I realize that denying myself things like my mom's cookies is extreme. I'm trying to be more reasonable with myself."

Jess says *I deserve dessert* to herself many times a day.

"It helps to think that I *deserve* a cookie, or a piece of banana bread, or whatever if I want one. I mean, everyone does. Thinking that I *deserve it* makes it feel more normal. It makes me feel less scared.

"It's weird, when I tried not to eat any sweets, I ate more. I mean I told my friends I stopped eating sweets, but I was lying. I ate a lot sometimes. I think I actually do eat healthier now because sweets aren't forbidden food; like the article said, if you know you can have a dessert, you'll eat healthier during the day. That's true for me. I don't have too much junk during the day—maybe some chips or fries at lunch, and that's usually it. But I do always have my dessert! I deserve it!

Jess found a way to help reinforce her Special Statement.

Action Plan

Sharing with a Friend

ess talked to a good friend about feeling upset about her weight gain, and she learned that her friend was going through the same thing.

"It helped knowing that when my good friend gained seven pounds in a couple of months, her doctor told her what my doctor told me—she's still growing, and that's why she gained the weight. My friend said her doctor told her that girls need some body fat—not too much, but some. She said the fat produces hormones so we can get our periods. So I guess we girls are all in the same boat. We have to have some fat to be normal. I hate that idea, but I wouldn't want to lose my period, either. My friend and I support each other. We remind each other that we both *deserve dessert!*"

Here's another idea that helps support Jess's Special Statement. Jess got this idea from her good friend, and now it helps her when she worries too much about her weight. Maybe it will help you, too!

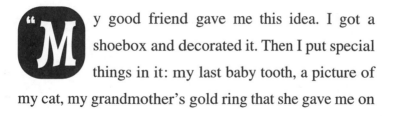

Action Plan

A Comfort Box

"My good friend gave me this idea. I got a shoebox and decorated it. Then I put special things in it: my last baby tooth, a picture of my cat, my grandmother's gold ring that she gave me on my tenth birthday. When I feel like I'm too fat, I look at the things in my comfort box, and it makes me feel better, like I have something special to think about. It helps me get my mind off my weight. It distracts me, and distraction is good! And my grandma was such a good baker, like my mom, so it helps me feel all right about *deserving dessert.*"

 Special Statement:

> ## "I'm strong, not fat."
> –Brandi, age 14

Brandi is an only child. She loves soccer and has played since first grade. Brandi even changed the spelling of her name so it's like Brandi Chastain, the U.S. women's soccer star. This year Brandi was picked to play on the junior varsity soccer team, even though she's just a freshman. She was excited, but the only bad thing is that her parents work long hours and can't be at her games very often. Brandi wishes her parents didn't have to work so much. And sometimes she wishes that she had an older brother who could tell her how to act around boys.

Brandi is really tall for her age—most of the kids in her

class come up to her shoulders. She is also muscular and strong. Although she feels good about excelling at sports (besides being good at soccer, she's the best long jumper in her class), Brandi has secretly always wanted to be like her best friend, who is totally unathletic, but is tiny and petite.

"I weigh a lot for my age, and my friends all weigh, like, eighty-five pounds. Sometimes I wish I was them. I'm never happy with my weight, but I know I'm just not built like them. I'm an athlete, and if I were skinny I wouldn't have my strength and endurance. I wouldn't be in good shape. I know there's not much I can do about it, but sometimes all I can think about is how big I am compared with everyone else. All my friends are little, and I feel like a big, fat elephant. It hurts."

One day Brandi realized that she was spending so much time worrying about her weight that she wasn't having any *fun!*

"I was out at the mall with my friends, and we stopped for pizza. But all I ordered was a diet cola. I just felt too fat to get anything else. One of my friends looked at me and said, 'You always get pizza, remember? You like pepperoni best. Why aren't you getting any pizza? That's no fun.' And I realized she was right. It wasn't fun ordering just a diet cola when everyone else was having pizza. It was terrible. I was sort of punishing myself. But I felt like I was so much bigger than everyone that I shouldn't eat anything.

"Then I asked my best friend if she thought I was fat. She said, 'No, you're strong, but you're not fat. You're the best athlete I know.' So that became my Special Statement: *I'm strong, not fat.* I say that to myself a lot.

"Thinking so much about my weight made me sad and worried all the time. I was scared to have pizza or french fries or anything with fat in it. Now I try to concentrate on having a good time. When I eat with my friends, I try to remind myself that I'm being normal. I think it helps me feel better about myself. And I really do kick butt on the soccer field!"

Brandi's Special Statement helps her turn her attention away from bad body-image feelings and put it toward having a good time with her friends. When she thinks to herself, *I'm strong, not fat,* it interrupts the miserable cycle of always feeling too big, so she can relax and enjoy her life.

Here's a creative idea that helps Brandi put her Special Statement into action.

Dancing Queen

"**I** like to dance to my mom's old music, disco music from the '70s or '80s, or any music, really. I made myself a dance playlist for my iPod. It's so stupid, but it's fun. When I feel fat and I make myself dance to stupid music, I just feel better. I don't know how else to say it. I feel free and crazy, but it takes my mind off myself, off thinking I'm fat. I just go into my room and close the door. I look really goofy, but who cares? There's no one but me, and I'm just being hyper and having fun. And honestly, after about three songs I'm okay about my body again—I feel *strong, not fat!* I got this idea because I read that lots of athletes dance to stay limber and flexible. Dancing makes me feel a lot better about my body. And it really is fun."

Special Statement:

"Get back to where you once belonged."

–Lindy, age 15

L indy describes herself as "very average: average grades, average looks." This is hard, because she feels that everyone else in her family is a genius: school comes easily to her older brother, and her parents are both professors. But all in all, Lindy gets along okay with everyone in her family.

When she was twelve, Lindy became obsessed with carbs. She thinks it's because her mom and dad were on a low-carb diet at the time, and all of a sudden there was never any bread on the dinner table. This gave her the idea that carbs are "bad." One night when her family ordered Chinese take-out dinner, Lindy said she only wanted plain chicken without any rice. She wouldn't touch her brother's fried rice, even though they always used to share an order. The next week, Lindy stopped eating bagels for breakfast. She wasn't exactly sure what a "carb" was, but at one point she threw up because she was afraid she had eaten too many of them.

Then one day last year at lunch, Lindy's best friend, Lisa, caught her picking the topping off her pizza and throwing the crust into the garbage.

"Lisa asked me what in the world I was doing. I told her I just couldn't eat carbs anymore. I even told her about the one time when I threw up. Lisa was really upset about that and said if I didn't tell my mom, she would. She told me I had to tell my mom, because even if I didn't know it, I had a problem.

"So we both told my mom together, Lisa and I. I was really scared to tell my mom about the throwing up. But my mom said, 'Okay, let's try to stop this before it becomes a bigger problem.' We went to my pediatrician. She said I had the beginning of bulimia and anorexia, and she gave us the name of a counselor.

"I've been talking to my counselor for almost a year, and I see a nutritionist, too. At first I talked mostly about being afraid that I would get fat if I ate carbs. But I learned that all carbs aren't bad for you, and I learned what's healthy, like fruits and vegetables and whole grains, and what's not, like junk food. And I learned that it's okay to eat *some* junk food. My nutritionist said if you eat healthy foods about 70 percent of the time, that's good. You don't have to be perfect.

"My nutritionist said that a baked potato is good to eat after school because it has something in it that makes you feel happier and gives you more energy. So even though it's a carb and it was kind of scary, I tried it. I think it does work— I felt better, and I could concentrate on my homework better. Now that's my everyday after-school snack! I feel proud of myself because I really do feel okay about eating it. My mom got potatoes, and I just put them in the microwave after school. It takes about five minutes to cook. The nutritionist said to eat the skin because that's good for you, too. She also said not to have a lot of diet soda because that can make you crave sweets."

During one of her counseling sessions, Lindy talked about what kind of person she was before she was afraid to eat carbs. She thought back to sixth grade—she felt fine about her body then. She really didn't think much about it. Life seemed a lot freer then. Lindy remembered that she ate junk food, but she also ate healthy foods, too. She remembered that she ate lots of fruit, and pretzels were her favorite snack.

"Then my counselor said that she wondered what's different in my life now, besides the fact that I'm afraid to eat carbs. I thought about it, and I realized that my life is so much harder now. School is stressful, and my friends have changed about four times since then. I started fighting more with my mom. And I'm worried about college and things like that, even though it's a couple of years away. Everything seems like it's going so fast, so out of control.

"My counselor asked me this: 'When you don't eat carbs, does it make you feel more in control?' I thought about that, too. At first I didn't understand what she meant, but now I think I do. I think instead of dealing with how out of control I feel, because that makes me feel really anxious, I focus on controlling my food. My counselor said that's what we have to talk about—how I can feel like I have more control in my life without worrying so much about carbs."

Lindy's progress has been up and down, but she's gradually learning to eat healthier, and she's finding more positive ways to feel in control.

"One thing that happened was that I worked really hard on an English paper but I only got a C+. I thought I would get an A. But my counselor said if I did my best, then that's all I could do. I didn't have control after that.

"We decided I could talk to my teacher to see what I could have done better. I did, and it helped. I got a C+ because of spelling mistakes, but she let me fix them and then she gave me a B-. And next time I'll check my spelling, so I can get a better grade, maybe even an A. Talking to my teacher helped me feel more in control—in a good way."

Lindy thought of her Special Statement one day in the car on her way to a piano lesson.

"We had the oldies station on because that's what my mom likes. I like it sometimes, too. And there was this Beatles song that said, 'Get back to where you once belonged.' And I thought, *that's just how I feel. I want to get back to feeling fine about my body and not worry about what I eat, like when I was in sixth grade.* Well, I'm more mature now, and I don't want to eat so much junk food like I did then, but I think you know what I mean.

"So now it's my Special Statement. I say, *Get back to where you once belonged* a lot to myself, and I think it helps. It makes me remember that I wasn't always so obsessed with carbs, and that I can be like that again. And I want to be—it's just really hard. But I'm trying. I can eat some carbs now, and I don't throw up anymore. I think I'll get there eventually."

Here's another idea that helps support Lindy's Special Statement.

Action Plan

Knowledge Is Power

Lindy was curious about eating disorders, so she decided to write a paper on anorexia nervosa and bulimia for English. Lindy learned some things that have had a positive, powerful effect on her body image.

"I learned all about eating disorders, which was interesting because I'm sort of going through that. But I also learned something else that was interesting. In the Fiji Islands, the girls never had eating disorders until they saw American TV, and now because they watch shows like *Baywatch,* they have eating disorders. This made me think about myself: do I let the media make me feel bad about my body? I think magazines do have a bad effect on me. But since I wrote my paper, I'm trying not to let them make me feel so bad. Actually, I'm trying not to read magazines that make me feel that way. I'm trying to treat myself and my body image better. I'm trying to *Get back to where I once belonged.*"

Getting the Picture

Jess, Brandi, and Lindy all had their special fears about food and weight. Jess was afraid that her weight gain—which is normal for teen girls, especially when you're still growing—meant that she was fat. Brandi felt bad about her body because she was taller and more muscular than her friends. Lindy got the idea in her head that carbs are bad and would make her fat, so she avoided them entirely—and this almost cost her good health.

All three girls used their Special Statements to try to be healthy and deal with their worries about food and weight.

When Jess read the article in the magazine, she decided that she *"deserved dessert,"* and then she was able to calm down and enjoy her mom's cookies as one of her basic human rights! Jess found other ways to put herself at ease when she worried about food and weight: She found solace in commiserating with her good friend and also used her comfort box to soothe herself. She discovered that when she allowed herself dessert, she actually ate healthier than when she was so tense and anxious about sweets.

Brandi's friends helped her understand that she was *"strong, not fat."* This helped her gain a different, more positive feeling about her body—especially about her athleticism. She also discovered that dancing around in her room was a great body-image boost!

Lindy realized that she had to stop obsessing about food or she would become seriously ill. She talks about her feelings with her counselor and is learning to cope with her problems so that she doesn't have to control her carbs to feel in control of her life. Also, Lindy gained some knowledge and insight when she wrote her paper on eating disorders and developed a healthy plan with her nutritionist: all this is helping her to slowly *"get back to where she once belonged."*

So be creative! Try some of these solutions for yourself.

Find a Special Statement that will help you sweep away *food and weight negativity* from your brain. Instead, look for your *positivity,* or good, self-accepting thoughts and feelings and activities. Worries about food and weight may have snatched them from you, but only temporarily. Be your own detective and find them again!

Here are seven good questions to ask yourself as you search for your *positivity:*

1 What do you love to do?

2 If you were on a desert island, what and whom would you take with you?

3 What song do you love? Why?

4 What movie makes you feel really warm and sentimental? Why?

5 What's the hardest thing you've been through, and how did you get through it?

6 Whom do you look up to?

7 What kind of person do you want to be in five years?

These are good places to start as you search for your positive thoughts and feelings about yourself and your body and your life. Then think of a Special Statement all your own.

Once you think of your Special Statement, let it work for you. Let it distract you from thinking 24/7 about food and weight. Let its positive idea fill you up and replace your worries.

Your life will feel a little fuller and a little brighter.

And your *body image* will be better, too!

3

The Catwalk in the Halls:

When School's a Big Fashion Show

The bell rings, and she gets butterflies in her stomach. She picks up her new purse—she used all of her birthday *and* Christmas money to buy it. Next, she stands and hopes everyone notices her new designer jeans. She tucks her hair behind her ears, so her new dangly earrings stand out. She feels a tinge of regret and wonders if her T-shirt makes her look fat. Why didn't she wear the blue one—the one that her best friend told her was cool? She takes a deep breath. Then it's her turn to walk through the door.

Is she auditioning for a movie role? Is she on a fashion shoot for a teen magazine? Is she on a "go see" for a Broadway play?

No. And you've probably guessed. She's about to walk down the halls of her school. In fact, she's on her way to lunch and hopes that if she looks the part, the cool girls will like her outfit, and the boy she likes might talk to her—maybe she'll even be invited to a party over the weekend.

Do people act like this at your school? Statistically speaking, you may have experienced a scenario similar to this yourself—or know someone who has.

Being considered a fashionista—or at least attractive and fashionable—is important to lots of girls. According to recent research, teen shoppers spend more than 170 million dollars a year, and 40 percent of that is spent on clothing and accessories. Studies also show that 36 percent of teen girls consider designer jeans a status symbol, and 23 percent feel that clothing labels say the most about a person. This same study showed that 67 percent of girls between the ages of thirteen and seventeen bought clothes the last time they were at the mall, and 58 percent say their friends have the most influence over their tastes in clothing.

So it's no wonder that millions of girls feel judged by their appearance. At some schools, how a girl looks dictates who will—and who won't—talk to her. A girl may feel that if she doesn't have the "right" jeans, the "right" shoes, the "right" purse, the "right" everything, she'll be at the bottom of the popularity scale, and no one will want to be her friend.

And the stakes are high: Some of the "right" jeans cost more than $100! Some of the "right" purses cost that much, too. Some of the "cool," one-size-fits-most T-shirts are expensive—and really *don't* fit most girls.

And there's more to it: Teens and preteens—especially girls—are targeted by advertising companies. These companies know that today's girls love to shop! As a result of their research on girls' shopping habits, they know your favorite brands, your favorite celebrities, your favorite music—and they create ad campaigns geared just for you! This isn't necessarily a bad thing—some of the products pitched your way are fun and unusual and help you express your individuality. But some stuff may be unflattering, not very special, and way too expensive!

It's a double-edged sword for many girls: On one side, you may really want to buy something that everyone else has, no matter what it costs or how it looks on you. Shopping can be a fun thing to do with your friends—and it's fun to have new, trendy things. On the other side, you may question the sanity of spending so much money. You may resent the pressure to look like everyone else.

You may ask yourself:

* ❀ Why do I have to buy what everyone else buys?
* ❀ Why can't I shop according to my own tastes and my own realistic budget?
* ❀ Why can't I just wear clothes that flatter me?
* ❀ Why does my appearance matter so much?"
* ❀ Why can't I be liked for who I am, period?
* ❀ What do I do if I can't afford to buy stuff like my friends can?

❀ **Even if I can afford it, what do I do if I think it's stupid to spend so much money on things I really don't need, or things that don't look good on me, just to follow the crowd?**

Some people may think that these questions are shallow and trivial, but there's nothing wrong with wanting to be in style. There's nothing wrong with wanting to express yourself with clothes and shoes and purses and jewelry. There's nothing wrong with experimenting with your hair and makeup. Finding your own style with fashion can be fun and creative— when you also follow your own sensibilities.

Here are the stories of three girls who have found ways to walk down their school halls with confidence, individuality, and style—without spending a lot of money. Did they need to change their image? Did they need to change friends? Did other people reject them for their new attitudes? Did they *really* feel attractive and accepted as they marched to their own fashion drum?

Read on. You'll see that all in all they really didn't have to do a radical makeover. They just had to start being more true to *themselves.*

"Fifteen a week for ME!"

-Suzy, age 15

Suzy is the only girl in a family of seven. Her four brothers don't care about clothing labels or stores or fashion trends. They let their mom buy clothes for them—they don't care very much about the color of their T-shirts or the style of their jeans.

Suzy cares a lot. She's happy that her brothers don't care about clothes—she thinks that means there's more money for *her* clothing allowance. Her parents do not share this opinion.

"I love fashion. I never have enough clothes. My mom will buy me two new outfits and a pair of shoes for school, and that's it. She says it's more than her mom ever bought her, but I don't think that's fair. The world's a different place, and fashion is important to me. It lets me express myself. I need more clothes than my mom, and she doesn't get this."

Suzy has an after-school job at a coffee shop. Her parents want her to save money for college, but it's been hard for her to cooperate. At one point, she was spending *all of her paycheck* at the mall. She bought new stuff every week, so she didn't have anything leftover for her college savings account.

She couldn't even afford to rent a movie once in a while—all her cash went to buying clothes!

"My dad and mom really came down on me. They said college is expensive, and if I want to go away to school, I really have to start thinking about saving money. Not just think about it—I have to save it. They said it's reasonable to save half my paycheck and spend the rest. I don't see it that way—college seems so far away. They took away my debit card, and that upset me. We just don't see eye to eye on this."

Then something happened, and Suzy started to see her parents' point of view. She was even inspired to change her shopping habits. Now she has a college savings account with money in it—and cool clothes, too!

"The timing of this is so weird. My parents were yelling at me for spending a lot of money on a purse. Then my friend Emily called, and I went to her house to see her and her cousin Ellen, who just graduated from college. Ellen is a lot older than Emily, but they're really close. And Ellen loves fashion like we do. She used to go to places like Neiman Marcus and Saks. She always looks perfect.

"Anyway, Ellen ended up charging over eight thousand dollars on her credit card the last year she was in college. She got scared because she didn't have a job and couldn't pay the bill. She was afraid her credit rating was ruined. She was lucky, because her dad paid off her credit card. He said it was her graduation present, but he'd never do it again. If she was irresponsible again and ran up her credit card, she'd have to find a way to pay her own bill. Ellen said all those clothes didn't make her happy anyway. She got bored with them and gave them away to her friends—and then she just bought more. She told us to learn from her mistakes and not to be stupid like she had been."

Suzy thinks this story forced her to be honest with herself about her own spending. It made her stop and think about her nonstop shopping. It made her wonder *why* she bought so many clothes that she didn't really need.

"It shook me up in a good way, I guess. I could see myself getting into the same situation, and I didn't want to be like that. My parents wouldn't bail me out if that happened to me! They'd be so pissed! They'd say 'I told you so' and something like I made my bed and now I have to sleep in it—they always say things like that. So Ellen made me see that I did have to change, so I didn't end up like her. Because I love clothes so much, I was heading in that direction. I could see that.

"I thought buying all this stuff would make me cool. It would make me special. It would make me fit in with all the girls who get credit cards from their parents. But like Ellen said, buying all that stuff doesn't make you happy. Emily and

I talked about this, and we agree. If people like you, they'll like you even if you don't spend as much money on clothes as they do. I hate to admit it, but my parents were just trying to help me. I can see that."

Action Plan

Suzy's New Concept: A Budget!

Suzy never used a budget when it came to spending her money. If she had money in her pocket, she spent it. And she never thought to shop at discount stores. But now her attitudes and behaviors are changing. Suzy and her parents sat down and designed a clothing budget—and she even thought of a Special Statement to help her stick to it!

"I'm lucky; I have a job, so I make around a hundred dollars a month after taxes. I do have to pay for my spending money in college, but besides my clothes and movies, that's about all I have to pay for. A girl in my math class said she has to pay for everything, even her school lunches.

"If I save ten dollars a week for college, that still leaves fifteen a week for me. That's what I think is fair.

My parents and I compromised on that one—I am saving less than half my paycheck, but they said if I save ten dollars every single week, no exceptions, they'll go along with it. I agreed to that. So I made *Fifteen a week for ME!* my Special Statement. It helps me remember that I can't buy everything all at once.

Suzy's Special Statement helps keep her on track, so she doesn't go crazy in stores like she used to. Here's how she puts *Fifteen a week for ME!* into action.

Action Plan

Smart Shopping–Suzy's Real Deal!

uzy learned that being smart about shopping leads to smart clothes at smart prices!

"I used to refuse to shop at discount stores. I was such a snob. My ideas were ridiculous: If things went on sale, they weren't any good because no one wanted them. I thought it was sad when things went on sale. I don't know where I got that idea—it sure wasn't from my parents. Ellen said that even celebrities shop at cheap places—she said some actor got a designer shirt for ten dollars at a thrift shop! She

said that stores like H&M and Target have good stuff—
and the prices are right. Now I realize how stupid I was.
Now I only buy clothes on sale or at discount stores or
resale shops. I get very cool clothes that way and very
cool deals! And I also keep to my *Fifteen a week for
ME!* budget.

"At first I was scared I wouldn't look good if I didn't
buy new stuff all the time. I was afraid I'd feel bad and
other people would change their opinion of me.
Everyone thought I was so fashionable—some of the
girls even copied me when I wore something trendy! I
was afraid my friends would give me a hard time if I
didn't buy everything like I used to.

"But that didn't happen. My two best friends even go
sale shopping with me! Their parents tell them they
need to stop spending so much, too. We checked out a
new resale shop in our city, and it was amazing. I got
four sweaters for fifteen dollars, and I think one may
have been part cashmere—it was really soft. I think I
look okay. I had to find a way to express myself and not
spend all of my money, and I think I've done that.

"*Fifteen a week for ME!* works for me: it's a good
Special Statement and a good budget. It's sort of like a
game. If I want a skirt, where can I get it the cheapest?

If I can find a leather jacket for twenty-five dollars at the Salvation Army instead of one hundred dollars at the department store, and fifty-dollar tops on sale for ten dollars, well, it's sort of fun. And I should be able to save and still afford to buy clothes—and movies, too. And if I really want something that would take me too long to save for, well, I could ask for it as a birthday or Christmas present.

Suzy thinks part of her spending problem has to do with the community in which she lives.

"Not all my friends are like this, but three girls in my group get a lot of money from their parents. My parents have enough money. We're pretty comfortable, but they're strict with me: They expect me to work and pay for stuff myself. They tell me they want me to know the value of a dollar. They also have to pay for college for five kids, which is a lot. Most of my friends only have two or three kids in their families.

"One of my friends got a credit card—that's a real status symbol at my school. When we go to the mall she can buy whatever she wants. Last weekend she bought a little Coach backpack. I couldn't believe it! She's a really nice girl, but I was so jealous. She told me that everyone is different, and her parents just let her spend a lot on clothes and purses. I wish that was me, but unfortunately it's not my life."

Suzy thinks that there's one good thing about having a budget: it helps her feel more in charge of her life.

"I was very out of control. I was always worried that something was too expensive, but I bought it anyway. I thought because it was *my* money, I could buy whatever I wanted. And I thought that if I didn't spend money like some other girls do, well, that would mean I'm not cool. But then I thought that maybe the cool thing to do is save some money for college, like I'm supposed to.

"And I don't fight so much with my parents anymore. My mom even treated me to a new pair of jeans because they were only ten dollars at a resale shop! And they were really cool jeans—I got lots of compliments, and I loved telling people I got them for ten bucks!"

Special Statement:

"I'm a creative chick, not a carbon copy."

—Alison, age 15

Alison doesn't have any brothers or sisters. Her parents are divorced, and she hasn't seen her dad in three years.

Alison's mom works two jobs to keep her in a Catholic high school. Needless to say, money is tight. But still, Alison loves clothes. She loves color and design. She loves to pair unusual pieces together to make a really unique outfit. When she graduates from high school, Alison wants to go to art school and major in fashion design.

Because she wears a skirt and blouse uniform, Alison doesn't worry much about being fashionable in school. She might roll down her socks or tie a ribbon around her neck or wear colorful earrings to feel special, but her creative choices are limited during school hours. However, the girls at her school *really dress up* for dances—one of the major times to socialize with boys—and this is where Alison's fashion problems began.

"Last year when I was a freshman, all the girls were getting manicures and pedicures and all that girly stuff for the Spring Fling dance. My friends all got new dresses and matching shoes and purses. They each got to spend around two hundred dollars on the dance. My mom said if I want to go, I could spend only fifty dollars. This was very depressing to me. My friends kept asking if I wanted to go with them to get their hair and makeup done. They just didn't understand that I couldn't go, that I had to do my own hair and makeup."

Alison wanted to go to the dance more than anything, but she worried a lot about how she would look.

"I felt really bad. I felt that if I went, I'd look really stupid. I could have borrowed a dress from my cousin, but she's not my size. I tried it on, but it was way too short, and it was too big in the bust and too small in the hips and waist. I felt very stupid in that dress, and I could barely breathe in it—I looked terrible. I had no idea what I would wear—I didn't have anything."

Alison almost didn't go to the Spring Fling.

"I was ashamed of my life. I didn't want to look like a dork. I was embarrassed about my mom because she doesn't make very much money, even though she's the greatest mom. The guy I liked was supposed to be there, and I was afraid I'd look stupid, and he wouldn't even talk to me.

"I just wanted to be like everyone else. My mom said she understood—she wishes she could drive a Volvo station wagon like her friend drives, but she can't afford it. Mom said it's okay to wish for something more, but we all have to deal with our own circumstances. She said lots of successful people come from families without a lot of money. She said that I'll have a better life someday because I'm a hard worker, and I'll go to college and have a career."

So this was Alison's reality: if she got a new dress, it would have to cost next to nothing. She felt a little pessimistic—she knew it would be practically impossible to find anything affordable in the department stores. But then Alison's mom reminded her of three of her best fashion qualities: her *good eye,* her *creative edge,* and her *sewing skills!*

"My mom told me I'm very creative, and she said she knew I would put something together that would be cool. So I decided that she was right. I decided I'd wear a pretty dress, and it would fit me perfectly—and I'd make it myself!"

"I thought of my Special Statement then—*I'm a creative chick, not a carbon copy.* Because I *am* creative, and I *don't* want to be a carbon copy! I went to the fabric store and found a beautiful remnant of designer material on sale for five dollars a yard. It was dark electric blue, and my eyes are blue, so it was definitely *my* color. I needed only three or four yards, so I could afford it, plus some shoes to match!

"My dress was perfect for me. It wrapped around and sort of looked like a sari. It was different from everyone else's dress, and I liked that. My mom did my hair in an updo, and she put flowers in it. I felt beautiful—and the boy I like told me I looked really good. By the way, he's my boyfriend now!"

Here's another way Alison feels like a uniquely fashionable *creative chick*—for very little money. This plan gives Alison and her best friend lots of ideas for creating their own special styles.

It's in the Bag

"**M**y best friend and I are both *creative chicks*. We love fashion, but we can't afford designer stuff. So we play a game we call 'Rich and Glamorous.' We go into an expensive store and ask for a shopping bag with the store logo on it. Sometimes they say no, but sometimes the salesperson is nice and gives us one. Then we put something in the bag—one of our own sweaters or something like that, and put tissue paper over it.

"So then we just walk in and out of expensive stores. We look at clothes and even try some on and get fashion ideas. The salespeople are usually nice to us—I think because they see we've 'shopped' somewhere expensive. We are also polite and thank them before we leave, like I saw some other girls do. So at the end of the day, even though we haven't bought anything, we've tried on clothes and we've gotten ideas about how to get the same look for cheap. It's really fun."

"Elegance is refusal."

–Emily, age 14

E mily is a late developer. She's still uncurvy in places where all her friends are curvaceous—no hips, no bust, and no bottom. She's also short and worries that everyone thinks she's still in middle school, even though she's a freshman in high school. Her mom was little when she was a teenager, too, but now she is average height and has a great figure. Emily's mom told her that the same thing will probably happen to her. But Emily still feels frustrated by her lack of height and curves.

"I want to wear what the other girls are wearing, but things like little T-shirts make me look like a little boy. Or I get lost in some styles, like those pretty prairie skirts. All the girls wear the cutest styles, but none of them look good on me. I don't feel like I fit in when I'm at school because all the girls look great except for me."

Emily felt terrible about her body. She didn't like the fact that she was still so small. Sometimes the boys would make fun of her and call her a munchkin, and that really hurt.

One day, which Emily calls "the worst day of my life so far," a mean girl told a boy Emily liked that she hadn't gotten her period yet. Emily was so embarrassed she called her mom and begged her to pick her up from school. Her mom said no, which upset Emily because she didn't want to see the boy in the halls. All this drama and stress gave Emily a terrible stomachache, and she spent most of that day in the nurse's office.

"I felt so bad, my stomach was very nauseous. I just couldn't go to class. Then my good friend stopped in to see how I was doing, and she told me that the boy didn't even listen to that mean girl; he said he hates her because all she does is stir up trouble between people. That made me feel a little better."

Emily was bored in the nurse's office. She noticed a teen magazine on a coffee table and began reading a cover story titled "Accentuate Your Positives." This article actually included a girl who was little and thin—and who, like Emily, hadn't developed her figure yet!

"Usually these articles are all about how to look slimmer. But this one had a girl who was tiny like me. It talked about what kind of clothes she should wear and what kind of jeans look best on girls who are little. I realized I *could* find my own 'look'—that I *could* find things that make *me* look good and more my age. It made me feel good to see that I'm not the only one with this problem."

Emily was excited about this article. She wanted to find *her own* special style, and she hoped her mom would buy her some new clothes, which her mom did. Then her mom told Emily something her own mom used to say, and this made Emily think of her Special Statement.

"My grandma told my mom that a long time ago a famous lady named Diana Vreeland said, 'Elegance is refusal.' My grandma liked that quote, and my mom does, too. I like it a lot, and now it's my Special Statement because it reminds me that I don't have to go along with everyone else. If something doesn't look good on me, I can refuse it and find something else. And I like the idea of looking 'elegant,' especially at my size! Looking elegant is the opposite of looking like a little girl, at least to me.

"The article said girls who are little and thin should layer. I love layering! It also said not to wear boot cut jeans, because if you're short, they make you look like you're standing in a bucket. Girls who are small should wear straight leg jeans, so I bought a pair, and I think they do make me look taller. Last week I put on my favorite jeans and a long T-shirt with another T-shirt in a different color over that; then I added a thin sweater. I wore a belt over everything. I don't look so thin with all those layers. And I feel good because layering is 'in' right now—maybe layering will always be 'in' for me! I felt cool when I wore that outfit to school—like I finally fit in, but in my own way. One of my friends even gave me a fashion compliment—she said she loved my layered look!"

Here's a tip from Emily that helps put *Elegance is refusal* into action.

Action Plan

Find a Skilled Person Who Can Do Alterations for Elegance–and That Could Be You or Your Mom!

The sleeves on Emily's jackets are always too long. So are the legs of her pants. Emily pins the hems up sometimes, but she had never taken the time to have her clothes properly tailored so that they would fit her small physique well.

"The article said that shortening sleeves is just as important as shortening hems. It makes your outfit look in proportion. My mom's good at sewing, so we're going through my clothes, and she's tailoring them to *my* measurements. I don't know why, but this is something I never thought about before. I would just buy clothes and roll up the sleeves, wear them, and feel bad because they never fit right. Now that my clothes fit me better, I feel like I have all these new dresses and jackets and pants and jeans—without spending more money!"

Getting the Picture

Suzy, Alison, and Emily all wanted to have a cool "look," but they all had certain constraints, just as most teen fashionistas do. None of the girls had carte blanche, or unlimited resources, for their wardrobes. But they all found ways to express themselves with their clothes, and they all look and feel confident!

Suzy has a good source of income—her after-school job. Still, she had to make a realistic clothing budget for herself, which meant keeping her clothes spending to fifteen dollars a week. Smart shopping helps Suzy feel fashionable without breaking her budget, and her Special Statement, *Fifteen a week for ME!* helps her stay on track and in control. Plus, some of Suzy's friends have even joined her in her new money-saving shopping habits.

Alison has *major* money concerns, but she saw herself as a *Creative chick, not a carbon copy!* Her Special Statement reminds her that she can use her *creativity* to keep current with trends—and even design some of her own! Alison's sewing skills and sense of design propel her into looking and feeling beautiful on a budget, and she gets new fashion ideas when she plays "Rich and Glamorous" in expensive stores with her good friend.

Emily had to learn to *refuse* some trends—some of them make her look too small and young. But some, like layering, make her look fashionable and elegant! Emily's Special Statement, *Elegance is refusal,* reminds her to refuse the trends that don't flatter her body, and to accept the ones that do. And tailoring the clothes in her closet gave Emily a virtually new elegant wardrobe, practically cost-free! (Emily's mom tailored her clothes, but if you or your mom can't do this, find a professional tailor who can. Look under "Alterations" in your phone book; some dry cleaners do alterations, too.)

Would you like to look more fashionable on a budget? Use some of Suzy's money-saving shopping tips: check the newspaper for sales, and check resale shops!

Do you like to sew, like Alison? You can find simple patterns at a fabric store or the notions section of a department store—or make up your own patterns! (Can't sew but would like to learn? Check out classes at your local fabric store or park district—or ask your mom or a friend to teach you.)

Does your body type, like Emily's, dictate refusing certain trends? That's okay, just as long as you embrace the styles that flatter *your* figure!

Most important, if you love fashion, have fun with it! You don't have to be a carbon-copy dresser. You don't have to spend tons of money.

Think of a Special Statement that reflects the fashionista in *you*!

Then be creative!

Find costume jewelry that's cool and cheap!

Find accessories that are the right style and size—and price!

Find flattering clothes that feel comfy and "you"!

Dress to *express yourself*!

And enjoy your own special look!

Can I Please Exchange My Big Stomach and Thunder Thighs?

Dealing with Your Body Type

Why is it that when it comes to our bodies, we are so rarely satisfied with what we have?

Too many times a girl who is tall wishes she were petite. A girl who has a nice, shapely bottom wishes it were smaller. A girl who has a pretty, rounded tummy wishes it were flatter. A girl whose legs are strong and muscular wishes they were thinner. The list goes on and on.

Family genes give us the color of our eyes and the shape of our ears. They give us the color of our hair and whether it is curly or straight. Genes are also a big factor in our body types—they determine the following:

- ❀ Whether we have big or small bones.

- ❀ Whether we're naturally muscular or slender.

- ❀ Whether we're tall or short.

- ❀ Whether we have small or large breasts.

- ❀ Whether we store fat in our stomachs, thighs, bottoms, chests, or faces.

So the body-image big question is: Can a girl possibly feel okay about the body type that was passed down to her by her family?

You've probably noticed that body types are as diverse as trees or flowers or animals—there are so many kinds of bodies in your school, in your community, and in the world. And there's a scientific explanation for this: *Diversity*—including body-type diversity—is the game plan for all life. Diversity ensures the survival of our species!

Martha Hansen, chairman of the science department at Evanston Township High School in Illinois, puts it this way: "Each individual has her own, unique, special genetic combination—and this is important for the success of our species because it allows us to adapt to our changing environment. That's why it doesn't make scientific sense to try to label one body type as the ideal body type. This goes against the basic tenet that diversity is important for survival."

Our bodies are actually *programmed* for survival. That's why it's so hard to change what nature intended—including our body types.

For one thing, metabolism, or how the body breaks down and uses the energy it gets from food, is complicated. Metabolism is regulated by food intake, hormones, exercise, and genetics. Our metabolism changes as our bodies and lifestyles change, which is why adults have different body shapes than teenagers.

When we restrict food intake, metabolism slows down to conserve energy. It's as if our bodies say, "We're in starvation mode! We have to slow down to survive!" That's why extreme measures—crash dieting, overexercising, diet pills, and so on—never work in the long run. It never works to try to mold your body into a body type that is different from what nature intended.

And since extreme measures don't work, they can affect your body image and self-esteem in a negative way. For example, a girl may go on a strict low-calorie "diet" and still not lose very much weight. That's because her metabolism will slow down to try to make up for her lack of calories. This may make her feel frustrated with herself—and feel bad about her body type. And it's such a negative cycle. When a girl feels bad about her body type, she'll probably feel dissatisfied with her appearance in general. When she looks at herself in the mirror, she may *never* think she looks pretty. It will be hard for her *ever* to have a good body-image day.

Still, there are some things that we can change about our bodies. It's true, we can't control our height or where we store our body fat or the size of our skeletons. But we do have a say-so in some areas.

We *can* control whether we have too much or too little body fat, and we *can* control the strength of our muscles and our cardiovascular fitness. To do this, we have to *eat healthily,* which means eating a variety of foods, including all the food groups—yes, treats, too!—and not overeating or restricting food intake. *Exercising regularly* is important, too, which means at least twenty to thirty minutes (but—so you don't get obsessed—not more than sixty minutes) of activity—like jogging, walking on a treadmill, dancing around in your room, jumping rope, doing yoga—most days.

When we treat our bodies respectfully—when we don't overfeed or underfeed them, when we exercise regularly, when we get enough sleep, when we take good care of them—it's possible for something almost magical to happen: our bodies *won't* gain or lose too much weight, and we can begin to see that *we are our own perfect body shape,* just the way we are! When this happens, even girls who never thought they'd ever like their body types can feel the wonder of accepting—and trusting—their bodies.

And when a girl *can accept* the body type she was born with, she has a better perspective on her appearance. She's able to feel more attractive. She's able to see herself in a more positive light—a light that reflects the natural beauty of her body and herself. And that positive light makes her more attractive to others as well!

Luckily, there *are* thoughts and behaviors and Special Statements that can help you acknowledge the perfection of *your* natural body type.

Here are the stories of three girls who have learned to do just this. They try to be healthy and fit. They try to eat well and exercise regularly. They try to be their best selves—and to treat their bodies with respect. Let them help *you* learn to do the same!

 Special Statement:

"My legs are strong. My stomach is fine!"

—Alicia, age 16

A licia has a sister and a brother. Her mom is an accountant, and her dad is a high school math teacher. Alicia thinks she should get good grades in math because her parents are so good at it—but she barely got a C in geometry last year. In fact, Alicia has always felt bad about herself because math has never come easy to her. She thinks this affects her self-esteem.

"I guess the smart math genes missed me. My brother and sister are both great at math, but I just don't get it. My strong subject is creative writing. My dad's mom—my nana—is a writer, so I guess I got her writing genes."

However, Alicia *did* get her mom's body-type genes. In fact, all of the women on her mom's side of the family have larger than average, feminine, pear-shaped bodies, and Alicia is no exception. Like her mom and her grandma and her two aunts, Alicia has a small waist and very curvy hips and thighs.

Alicia has never liked her legs. Specifically, she hates her thighs. She wishes they were thin, like her younger sister's thighs. Alicia has felt this way ever since she was a little girl.

"I've always hated my thighs. My little sister has thin legs, and I'm mad that my thighs are so big. It's not fair. My brother's legs are bigger, but it doesn't bother him like it bothers me. He plays sports, so he thinks his legs are a positive. But I see mine as totally negative.

"I remember when I was in third grade my doctor was talking about maturing and stuff like that, and she asked me how my life was going. I told her that the only thing wrong was that I hated my legs because they're too fat. My doctor tried to tell me that my legs were not fat. She said that my legs were in proportion to my body. She said I was fine. But I wouldn't believe her. I was obsessed. I thought that when she told me my legs were in proportion to my body, she meant I had a fat body. It made me feel terrible, even though I know she was just trying to be nice.

READER/CUSTOMER CARE SURVEY

HEFG

We care about your opinions! Please take a moment to fill out our online Reader Survey at **http://survey.hcibooks.com.**
As a **"THANK YOU"** you will receive a **VALUABLE INSTANT COUPON** towards future book purchases as well as a **SPECIAL GIFT** available only online! Or, you may mail this card back to us and we will send you a copy of our exciting catalog with your valuable coupon inside.

(PLEASE PRINT IN ALL CAPS)

First Name _____ MI. _____ Last Name _____

Address _____ City _____

State _____ Zip _____ Email _____

1. Gender
☐ Female ☐ Male

2. Age
☐ 8 or younger
☐ 9-12 ☐ 13-16
☐ 17-20 ☐ 21-30
☐ 31+

3. Did you receive this book as a gift?
☐ Yes ☐ No

4. Annual Household Income
☐ under $25,000
☐ $25,000 - $34,999
☐ $35,000 - $49,999
☐ $50,000 - $74,999
☐ over $75,000

5. What are the ages of the children living in your house?
☐ 0 - 14 ☐ 15+

6. Marital Status
☐ Single
☐ Married
☐ Divorced
☐ Widowed

7. How did you find out about the book?
(please choose one)
☐ Recommendation
☐ Store Display
☐ Online
☐ Catalog/Mailing
☐ Interview/Review

8. Where do you usually buy books?
(please choose one)
☐ Bookstore
☐ Online
☐ Book Club/Mail Order
☐ Price Club (Sam's Club, Costco's, etc.)
☐ Retail Store (Target, Wal-Mart, etc.)

9. What subject do you enjoy reading about the most?
(please choose one)
☐ Parenting/Family
☐ Relationships
☐ Recovery/Addictions
☐ Health/Nutrition
☐ Christianity
☐ Spirituality/Inspiration
☐ Business Self-help
☐ Women's Issues
☐ Sports

10. What attracts you most to a book?
(please choose one)
☐ Title
☐ Cover Design
☐ Author
☐ Content

FOLD HERE

Comments

"I know that I shouldn't complain, because I'm healthy. I'll never be skinny. But I wish I was thinner, and I especially wish that my legs were thinner."

Alicia's mom told her that at one time in history their body type was considered the most beautiful type of body a woman could have. She reminded Alicia that many famous paintings in their local art museum are of voluptuous women that look alluring, soft, and feminine. In fact, Alicia's grandma was very curvy and always had boyfriends. But none of this helped Alicia's feelings.

"I know my grandma was a big girl in high school, and she was a guy magnet. I've heard that a million times. But I don't really care. Everyone wants to be skinny these days, and I do, too. I think I'd feel way prettier if I had thinner legs, but even when I lost some weight last summer when I had mono, my legs were still fat. I didn't really notice a difference."

One night during a sleepover, Alicia talked to her best friend about her negative feelings about her legs and thighs. Her best friend said something that made a big impression in Alicia's mind—and this led to her Special Statement.

"My friend said that she doesn't think that I have fat legs. She said she'd trade *her* legs and stomach for *my* legs and stomach any day. She said she has a big stomach and mine is flat and that my legs are really okay.

"I got it then: my best friend, who I think looks perfect, wishes she could change something about her body, too. Maybe everyone wishes that. But I thought to myself, *I would rather have my thighs than a big stomach.* I really do have a fairly flat stomach. For some reason I don't gain weight in my stomach. I store fat in my legs and hips. So I suppose I can see the positives in my body type. I guess I'm glad about that. So I decided to remind myself of the positives with my Special Statement.

"I also wanted to start exercising more—I thought maybe I could be fitter. So I asked my mom what was available in our community. She said we have a health club, but it's expensive, and a YWCA. I'm going to check out the Y, but in the meantime I've started running on the weekends. I'm up to two miles, and I always feel better about my body after I exercise. And one good thing about my legs—they're strong! I can run really fast!

"So that's my Special Statement—*My legs are strong. My stomach is fine!* And this makes me feel a little better. It helps my body image! It doesn't help me feel that much better about my legs, because I know they're not the greatest. But they're my legs, and they're my mom's family's legs, too. So I guess that's a little acceptance, right?"

Here's something that strengthens Alicia's Special Statement.

Checking Out the Pictures

One day after school, Alicia looked at a scrapbook with her camp pictures from the summer before fifth grade. She was fascinated with what she saw. There was a big picture of herself—she was standing on the beach in a bathing suit with four other girls. Alicia realized that she was a cute little girl. She was the same size as all the other little girls—and her legs were not fat at all!

"I remember I felt so bad about my body at camp. I thought my thighs were so fat, fatter than all the other girls'. And looking back now, I see that I was wrong. I had the wrong impression. My thighs were normal, just like a little kid's thighs. They weren't any fatter than anyone else's.

"I'm going to try to remember this picture the next time I obsess about my fat legs. I'm going to think of it when I say to myself, *My legs are strong. My stomach is fine!* Maybe if I can remember that my thighs really weren't fat then, I can accept them better for how they are now. I mean, maybe they're really not as fat as I think they are now, either."

Special Statement:

> **"I love ME!"**
>
> –Jenny, age 14

J enny is the youngest daughter in her family, but she isn't the youngest child—she has two younger brothers. Her dad travels a lot for work, and her mom is a part-time librarian. Jenny gets along pretty well with her family. She makes dinner Tuesday nights, when her mom works late. Jenny likes this responsibility.

She also likes to knit. When Jenny was seven, her grandmother taught her how to knit, and now she knits whenever she can, especially when she watches television. Jenny puts her phone on "speaker phone" so she can knit and talk at the same time! Jenny feels proud because she made herself a pullover sweater last year. It's a pretty pinkish-coral turtleneck, and it looks really good on her. This is important because, as you will see, it is hard for Jenny to find sweaters that fit just right.

Jenny is fourteen, but more than one person has told her that she looks seventeen or eighteen. Jenny thinks this is because she has a very large chest for her age. This is a family trait—both grandmothers are big bosomed, and her mom is, too. Jenny's older sisters also have big busts. Jenny wishes she had inherited her Aunt Debbie's genes—Aunt Debbie is her father's sister, and she's the only woman in the family who has an average-sized bustline.

"When I was twelve, I was a 34C. Now I'm a 34DD. My weight is normal, but my boobies are huge! I hope this is as big as I'll get, but I don't know—my mom is a lot bigger than I am, and so is my grandma, her mom.

Jenny has thought about getting breast reduction surgery, but her mom said she's much too young for that. The reason that Jenny wanted a doctor to give her a smaller chest was so her clothes would feel better on her body.

"I can't get clothes to fit right. Regular T-shirts make my boobs stick out even more, then my lower stomach shows. My mom doesn't like that. And when a boy likes me, I think it's just because of my boobs, not me. It's very hard to deal with my boobs."

Jenny found her Special Statement one day when she was talking to her mom over lunch. She asked if her mom's breasts were big when she was fourteen. Her mom said they were, and she used to feel self-conscious about it. But then she got fed up with worrying about them and decided to accept her breasts as a part of herself. Jenny's mom decided to *love herself*, big breasts and all! If anyone made fun of her big breasts—well, she just wouldn't be their friend.

"This made sense to me. I mean, my mom sort of gave me permission to stop worrying so much about my boobs because *she* doesn't worry about hers. She said her boobs are part of herself, and she's happy with herself. I decided that my Special Statement should include the words I love me. So I just made that my Special Statement—*I love ME!* First, I thought, *Is this okay for a Special Statement?* It sounded like I was so full of myself. But my mom said it's okay because every girl should love herself.

"I think my Special Statement helps me not to think so much about my boobs and to just go on with my life. I mean, there's a lot more to love about me besides my big boobs!"

Here's one way Jenny supports her Special Statement.

Action Plan

Figure-Flattering T-Shirts

Jenny finally found some T-Shirts that really do look good on her.

"I went shopping with my mom—I hate going with my friends—and we found some clothes that make me look more normal. I got some long tank tops to put under my shorter T-shirts, and I got T-shirts that sort of skim instead of cling to my boobs. This makes me feel less self-conscious about my boobies because they don't stick out so much.

"Also, the saleslady told us that a V-neck or a square neck is good for girls with big chests, so my mom let me get a few new T-shirts of both kinds. They don't have really high or really low necklines—the V-neck isn't that low and the square neck one comes to just below my collarbone. And they don't show off my boobs either. No cleavage! Actually, these T-shirts really help a lot. They're not so tight, and I feel comfortable—and I'm still wearing a T-shirt like everyone else."

Here's something else that Jenny does to support her Special Statement, *I love ME!*

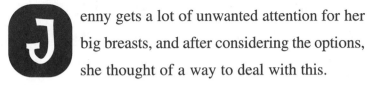

Action Plan

A Short Retort

Jenny gets a lot of unwanted attention for her big breasts, and after considering the options, she thought of a way to deal with this.

"I'm so sick of the boys making rude remarks. Once a boy tried to touch my boobs when I walked by him in English class. I was so mad and embarrassed. Guys whistle at me—even older guys I don't know, like

construction workers! It's true. Some men were working on our neighbor's house, and when I walked by on
the sidewalk, one of them whistled at me and said,
'Nice knockers.' I'm so sick of this. It's so disgusting.
And the more I think of my Special Statement—the
more I say to myself, 'I love ME!'—the more I feel this
way."

Jenny finally decided that she wanted to find a way to
give these people the message that she thought they were
stupid, idiotic, and pathetic, and that they should leave
her alone. She had lots of ideas about how to do this.

"First, I thought I could look the other way and pre-
tend I don't see them, but I tried it, and it didn't work.
Then, I thought I could yell at them, but my friend said
that that would only make it worse, and I agreed.
Finally, I thought of this: I could just tell them, 'You're
pathetic,' and walk on. So that's what I do now. And it
may not make them stop, but it makes me feel better.
Instead of feeling embarrassed about my boobs, I feel
like I have some respect for myself. I used to feel like
something was wrong with me, that I somehow
deserved these rude comments. But now I let them
know I think they're the pathetic ones, not me."

"I am who I am."

–Emma, age 17

E
mma is a great athlete. She's on the varsity tennis team, and she's a fast freestyle swimmer. She also plays golf and runs on the cross-country team. Emma received a tennis scholarship for college—it's the only way she is able to attend an out-of-state university. Emma's two older brothers didn't go to college after high school, and she's proud of the fact that she'll be the first child in her immediate family to pursue a higher education. Emma wants to study to be an architect, like her aunt.

Emma's dad is a marathon runner—he placed first in his age group in a recent race. Emma has her dad's body type: the body of an athlete. For Emma, this means that she has long, strong legs, small hips, small chest, and practically no waistline.

"My mom says my body is angular. I hate it. My weight isn't bad—I'm not too skinny, and I'm not fat. A lot of people think I look great. People always tell me I have an 'athletic look,' and they think I'm in such great shape. But I don't think I look great at all. I feel like my body shape is not normal. Maybe if my hips were bigger or my breasts were bigger it would help me look better, but I just feel like I don't look very feminine. I don't have curves like the other girls. I think I look like a guy. It's depressing to me."

Emma has tried exercise and weight training to create some curves, but this hasn't really helped as much as she wished it would.

"I thought if I did crunches, it would help me get a smaller waist. When I gain weight, I do gain it around my middle, so I thought crunches would help. But it really didn't help that much. Then I tried touching my toes and doing twists, but that didn't help much either. I tried strengthening my chest muscles because I thought I could get a little curvier on top, and it would look like I had a smaller waist. I think that maybe I got a little bigger, but it didn't really help my waist problem. That's what I feel like—like I have a big problem in an otherwise good life."

One day Emma had to get a sports physical, so she took the opportunity to talk to her doctor—she had *lots* of questions.

"I feel comfortable with my doctor; she's known me since I was a baby. I asked her some things that I've been wondering about: Is there something wrong with me? Do I have some kind of a hormonal problem? Aren't girls supposed to gain weight in their hips? Why don't I have a waist like all the other girls? I worry about these things a lot. I feel so unattractive and it hurts. I just wanted to know if there was anything I could do about it.

"My doctor said my height and weight are good. She said I don't have any hormonal problems—my periods are normal, and they wouldn't be if I did. She told me some athletes don't get their periods, which means they don't have enough body fat, but I'm fine. She said, 'You're built how you're built; your bone structure is what it is.' She told me everyone is built differently. She said hips are formed by the size of the bones and also how they're spaced. She said I'm built like a runner, like my dad. She told me not to worry about it because it is what it is, and there's really not much to do about it. That was hard for me to hear, but in a way it did help. That's when I thought of my Special Statement—because it's true—*I am who I am.*"

Like Jenny, Emma found that certain types of clothing supported her Special Statement and made her feel much more comfortable and confident. As a result, she was able to perceive her body type more positively—she was able to feel less self-conscious about her lack of a small waistline. And she felt, for the first time ever, a little *attractive.*

"I have a friend who knows all the latest styles, and she said the Empire waist is in style—it's a higher waistline that hits just under my bra. It's pretty—it's a feminine look. There are lots of tops now and even dresses that are the Empire style. So

I bought some long tops and short dresses, and I wear them with my jeans. The Empire waist hides my thick waist—it just skims over it. So I think I look much more feminine. It's a good feeling for me.

"My friend also told me to wear a skinny belt just above my waist so I look like I have curves. So I wore a sweater over my jeans and put a little belt on, and it looked better. It sort of looked like I had a waistline.

"Of course this is all an illusion, but it makes my waist look smaller, and it makes me look curvier, and that makes me feel better about my body. I know my Special Statement is *I am who I am,* but it's okay to get a little help sometimes! It's okay to wear clothes that you know cover up the areas you wish were different!"

Here's something else that Emma thinks about that bolsters her Special Statement.

Action Plan

What Can My Body Do?

 mma wishes she had a more feminine body type, but she realizes that her strong, athletic body can do things that lots of other girls can't do. This thought gives Emma a little body-image support.

"When I feel bad about my body, it helps to say to myself, 'I am who I am,' and then think of *all the things my body can do.* I'm good at sports. I'm a great snow-boarder. That's lots of fun, and I meet cute guys—they respect girls who can keep up with them. I helped my dad move a piano—that's how strong I am! I'm training to run my first marathon with my dad, and I know I'll finish because I have good endurance. These things make me feel special, and I am, I guess. Maybe my body is not as curvy as my friends', but then again, theirs aren't like mine, either. I mean, I'm so much bet-ter at sports and physical activities than they are. I win tennis competitions! And it's because I was born with this body. When I think about it this way, I can honestly say, *I am who I am,* and I like who I am, too!"

Getting the Picture

Do you dislike the size of your body? Do you wish your body shape was different? Do you think your body type is unattractive? Are you self-conscious about a particular body part?

Alicia, Jenny, and Emma answered yes to these questions: Alicia hated her thighs and legs, Jenny was uncomfortable with the size of her breasts, and Emma wanted more curves and a smaller waistline. Each girl has a different type of body, and each girl felt unhappy about the body type she was born with. And yet Alicia, Jenny, and Emma all found ways to calm down their negative body-type feelings. Their Special Statements and supportive actions help them accept their bodies and feel better about themselves.

Alicia didn't like the fact that she stored fat in her thighs and legs, but she was able to have a better body-type feeling after she talked with her friend. She realized that she didn't have thin legs, but she didn't have any problems with her stomach. She also learned an important fact: that even a girl who seems to "have it all" can feel unhappy about her body type. Her good friend, who looked beautiful to Alicia, said she'd trade her "imperfections" with Alicia any day! Looking at old camp pictures also helped Alicia put her bad body-image feelings into a more positive perspective—and reinforced her Special Statement, *My legs are strong. My stomach is fine!*

Jenny wished her breasts were smaller, like her Aunt Debbie's—and like most of her friends. And yet when she talked with her mom, she realized that it was okay to feel good about herself—and to say, *I love ME!*—big breasts and all.

She also found that flattering T-shirts helped her feel better about her body type and that she could deflect random rude remarks so that they didn't penetrate her better body image.

Emma understood her body was that of an athlete—angular instead of curvaceous—and that her athletic body type has its pluses and minuses. When she decided to value her body's very good qualities, such as strength and endurance—and the talent to win an athletic scholarship to college—it was easier to deal with her negative feelings about her waist. It was easier for her to say to herself, *I am who I am!* Also, like Jenny, Emma learned to choose clothing styles that drew attention away from the part of her body she was most self-conscious about.

Do you see your body type as unattractive and large instead of seeing the beautiful parts of yourself, such as your curviness, your strength, your personality? Or do you see your body type as unattractive and weak and small instead of seeing the beautiful parts of yourself, such as your delicateness, your petiteness, your personality?

Whatever type of body you have, whether you're large boned or tiny boned or, like most of us, somewhere in-between, your body type is part of the complex person that you are. You inherited your body type. It is part of yourself, just like your eye color or your personality or your experiences in life.

Your body type is special and unique. To accept it—and love it because it is part of *you*—is your birthright.

So try to *embrace* your body type.

Let yourself see its *positives* and *pretty points*; make them more important than the "negatives." And use them to think of your own Special Statement.

Dress to *highlight* the things you like about your body.

Feed your body with *healthy* food.

Get some *exercise.*

Respect your body type.

Build up some *trust* in your body type.

It is a part of the Beauty of You!

5

2 Hard 2 Be 2 Good:

Dealing with Perfectionism

Perfectionism is not a bad word. In fact, researchers have found that if you're a perfectionist, there can be plenty of *good things* about you!

Perfectionism can be defined as thoroughness, diligence, precision, and exactness. It gives you the energy you need to work hard. Perfectionism can help you persevere and attain a goal, even in the face of obstacles. It can help you stay focused and on task—and ultimately succeed!

Great artists, athletes, musicians, composers, teachers, writers, and scientists don't settle for mediocrity: think golfer Tiger Woods or classical violinist Sarah Chang. They are perfectionists and, as a result, are at the top of their fields. Many perfectionists, like biologist Luther Burbank or civil rights leader Martin Luther King Jr., have changed our world with their achievements!

Take this quiz:

1. I try my hardest in sports, even if I'm not the best on the team.

   ❑ TRUE   ❑ FALSE

2. If I don't get a good grade on a test, I study harder for the next one.

   ❑ TRUE   ❑ FALSE

3. I expect excellence from myself.

   ❑ TRUE   ❑ FALSE

4. I work hard to improve my natural skills, even if I already excel at them.

   ❑ TRUE   ❑ FALSE

If you answered True to any of the statements, you may be a perfectionist in a positive way!

But there is also another side to perfectionism.

A perfectionist may use her perfectionism in a *negative* way. She may expect herself to achieve goals that are unrealistic— and impossible! Intense anxiety may prevent her from *ever* feeling satisfied with herself, so when she fails to meet her own expectations, she may feel very upset and frightened inside.

Consequently, a negative perfectionist may never, ever feel smart enough, nice enough, attractive enough, or *good enough*. Many bright, talented girls fall into this category. A girl may feel an inner pressure to be perfect in *every aspect* of her life—the best student, the most talented athlete, the most compassionate friend, the prettiest girl, the most popular girl, and so on. And if she can't be the best, she may feel like she's the worst.

Or a girl may focus on one part of herself to perfect, which is often her body shape and eating habits. When a girl's body is the target of her perfectionism, she usually never feels that her appearance is acceptable. Negative perfectionism has been linked to low self-esteem, anxiety disorders, depression, poor body image, and eating disorders.

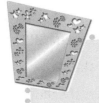

Now take this short quiz:

1. If I don't get a good grade on a test or paper, I feel embarrassed, stupid, and/or angry with myself.

   ❏ **TRUE**   ❏ **FALSE**

2. I usually don't raise my hand to participate in class discussions because I'm afraid I'll say something wrong or unintelligent.

   ❏ **TRUE**   ❏ **FALSE**

3. I'm very hard on myself when I make mistakes.

   ❏ **TRUE**   ❏ **FALSE**

4. If I think a girl looks more attractive than me, then I don't feel attractive.

   ❏ **TRUE**   ❏ **FALSE**

If you said True to any of these statements, you may have some negative perfectionism.

So if you're a negative perfectionist, how can you learn to turn the tables and be a positive perfectionist? How can you challenge yourself with high expectations and goals and still feel good about yourself, even if you can't meet them all? How can you accept your strengths—and your weaknesses— as the total, perfect package of *you?* The answer to these questions makes perfect sense: it's all about how you *use* your perfectionism.

As you learn to channel your perfectionism in a positive direction, instead of using it to punish yourself or put yourself down, you'll be able to pursue your goals with persistence and success. You'll be able to see that positive perfectionism isn't so much about never having a flaw or never making a mistake. Rather it's about working hard, following your passion, accepting support and constructive criticism from others, and having faith in yourself and your own special abilities.

Here are the stories of three girls who have learned how to direct their perfectionism in positive ways. They all use their Special Statements to turn self-criticism into self-acceptance and self-motivation. Try some of their ideas! See if they can help you to do the same!

"STOP the negative. GO for the positive!"

–Maggie, age 16

Maggie does well in high school and has always scored high on standardized tests. She is in a "gifted math" after-school program at a local university. Even though her friends think she's "got it all"—brains, beauty, and popularity— Maggie feels like they're all wrong. Specifically, she feels like she's definitely not pretty enough.

"My parents have high expectations for me. My mom is a nurse, and my dad is a scientist and a computer genius. They expect me to get good grades, and I do. I want to excel in school. But I wish my thighs were thinner. I wish I had a smaller nose. I know how to work hard and get good grades, but I want to be beautiful. At least I want to feel that way, but I don't at all."

Maggie feels both sides of her perfectionism. She uses it positively in school—she works hard and does her best. But she uses it negatively in regard to her body image. Maggie feels very anxious about her body—she *never* feels satisfied with her appearance.

"I begged my mom for a nose job. She said, 'No.' I started

jogging. I wanted to go on a diet, but my mom said, 'That's not a good idea.' She said, 'You need some fat on your body to be healthy,' and she told that me I'm not too fat at all. But that didn't help. I still felt miserable about myself because I could never look how I wanted to look. I felt like a failure."

Maggie's negative perfectionism was leading her down the hard road of poor body image. But then something happened, and she was inspired to look at herself within a different frame of mind.

"A girl in our school started to complain nonstop about her body. She kept asking people if she was fat. My friends and I wanted her to go away, but she was at our lunch table; she just went on and on about it. We ended up leaving and finishing lunch in the library. She was so annoying.

"But secretly, she was like a mirror to me. I could see myself—my negative side. I decided on my Special Statement because of her. When I say my Special Statement, I think of a *red light* when I say, *STOP the negative,* and I have that girl in mind, too. And I think of a *green light* when I say, *GO for the positive.*

"I say my Special Statement to myself when I feel like I'm fat or if I think everyone's prettier than me. It's a slippery slope for me. I can fall down it so fast, and then I feel really bad and ugly. But I just tell myself to *STOP the negative. GO for the positive!*

"It helps to tell myself to go for the positive because I think I do have more positives than negatives, even if the negatives feel really strong. My main negative is that I don't feel that pretty, so I do have a lot more positives: I have good friends, good parents, I'm smart, I'm okay at soccer—at least I have fun on the team. I don't always feel better when I remember all that, but I'm trying, and my Special Statement helps. I figured out if I keep being so perfectionistic about my appearance, I'll never feel good. And when I think about my positives, it helps me get my mind off not feeling pretty."

Here's something else that helps Maggie put *STOP the negative; GO for the positive!* into action.

Action Plan

A New Idea: Pretty Enough

Maggie wishes she looked like a model, like her good friend Tina.

"What can I say? Tina is tall and blond and thin. She has great hair and looks great in clothes. She has a beautiful face. Everyone talks about how pretty she is, even the teachers."

One day Maggie asked Tina what it was like to be so pretty. And Tina's response was a real eye-opener!

"Tina said that all she ever hears is how pretty she is. She said she doesn't even think she's that pretty. She thinks people are just saying that because she's not good at anything else—like she's only good at looking cute. She said someone even asked her if she was going to college, or to modeling school! They meant it as a compliment, but it hurt Tina's feelings. She wants to be a doctor."

Tina told Maggie that she wishes people would think of her as smart or good at basketball or a nice person. She said she'd be happy if people just thought she was "pretty enough."

"I thought about that. I think I'm probably pretty enough. I think I can accept that about myself. I know I'm not totally ugly. It's like I'm okay pretty, but not really pretty. I'm definitely not the prettiest like Tina. But then it would be creepy if the only thing anyone ever said about me was that I was pretty.

"Thinking about Tina helps me be a little less hard on myself. It helps me really mean it when I tell myself, *STOP the negative; GO for the positive!* This is weird, but I kind of feel bad for her. And I do feel good about myself for my accomplishments, even if I'll never look like her. Yesterday I told Tina that she was really one of my nicest, sweetest friends. She said that made her day."

⭐ Special Statement:

"Be rational!"
—Melly, age 15

Melly is a sophomore in high school. Her whole family is health conscious: her dad watches his cholesterol; her mom watches her weight and weighs herself every day; her sister, a year older, is a vegetarian. Melly has taken piano lessons since she was five, and her positive perfectionism has made it possible for her to perform in competitions, which she loves. Melly's negative perfectionism has to do with food: she's afraid to eat anything "unhealthy."

"No one eats junk at my house. We don't even have any—everything in the fridge is healthy: fruit instead of ice cream, things like that. The only chocolate we have is 70 percent chocolate bars, which my mom says are healthy, but I think they're gross—they're so bitter. I like milk chocolate better. Sometimes when I'm with my friends, I want a brownie like everyone else. Or I want a scone at the coffee shop. But then I feel so guilty when I eat it."

Melly's desire to eat healthily is a good thing—it's good to nourish ourselves with good, healthy food. But there's such a thing as *too much* of a good thing. And that's where Melly was heading—at full speed!

"I got obsessed. At one point, I thought if I ate one bite of a brownie, I screwed up my day. Then I just ate more brownies because, what the heck, the day was spoiled anyway. I felt so bad afterward. I felt very anxious. I thought about throwing up, but I didn't want to get into that. I didn't want all this to lead into an eating disorder.

"I talked to my mom about it, and she said I should talk to someone, like a counselor, and I agreed. I thought I had to eat perfectly, and I knew that was sick.

"Actually, I thought my mom was part of the problem because she talks about food and weighs herself all the time. My mom is so totally healthy. She brags about how she didn't keep on any of the weight she gained when she was pregnant. She makes a big deal about that. She says it's because she never eats junk. We never order dessert when we go out to eat because of my mom—she says things like 'Are you really going to eat that?' I know she means to be helpful, except it makes me so scared that I'll mess up. But I can't help it. Sometimes I do eat sweets. But then I hate myself."

Melly found a good counselor through a referral from her pediatrician. As they talked, Melly slowly realized that she was *stressing herself out* with her eating perfectionism. All it did was to make her feel bad and create drama in her life. She wanted to change, but it was hard to let go of her strict ideas about what she should and shouldn't eat. Many of Melly's ideas were irrational—but she'd had them practically all her life. She was used to worrying about her mom judging every morsel she put in her mouth!

Melly's counselor helped her identify her irrational thoughts about food. Then she helped her replace the irrational thoughts with rational, logical, self-respecting thoughts—thoughts that helped Melly quiet down her negative perfectionism.

"My counselor said that girls who are negative perfectionists have a lot of anxiety, and they feel like they need to be in control of everything—and that can lead to irrational thoughts and bad feelings. It was true for me. I was obsessed with controlling everything I ate. It wasn't logical, but I thought that was the way I should be. And I constantly felt terrible about myself.

"I think my most irrational thought is that if I eat one unhealthy thing, it will ruin my day, and I may as well just eat a lot of unhealthy things. When I talked about this with my counselor, she said that one brownie doesn't ruin anything, or one piece of cake, or one cookie—it's my *anxiety* about it that makes me think my day is ruined. So my rational thought is that if I eat a treat, it's okay, and it will all average out. It's not that many calories, and if I don't binge afterward, I'll be okay.

"Another irrational thought I had was that if I ate something unhealthy, it would make me gain weight right away. I could sort of feel the fat growing on me after I ate something like a piece of cake. But my counselor said that wasn't rational, because it takes more than a few minutes to gain weight.

"So I thought of my Special Statement. Whenever I get upset about eating something unhealthy, I just tell myself *Be rational!* and that does help me calm down. It helps to think of the logical side—it helps me to be able to go out with my friends and have a treat and not freak out about it so much."

Melly even got up the courage to talk to her mom about a few things.

"This was hard because my mom and I are close, and I didn't want to hurt her feelings. But I told my mom that I had to calm down about food, and I couldn't be so perfect. My mom was okay. She was worried about me and didn't want to make things worse for me. I told her that all her talking about what to eat and how much she weighs and her exercise makes me scared to eat anything that's not healthy. I told her it's not her fault, but I see her as perfect, and I see myself as a failure. And I told her I think she judges me and what I eat.

"My mom told me I don't have to eat perfectly—even she doesn't eat perfectly. And my mom said she'd try not to talk about food or her weight with me. I was happy about that. I still worry about what she thinks, but talking made me feel better."

Melly put her Special Statement into action with this plan.

A Rational Experiment

O ne day Melly talked to her counselor about how much she wanted to eat a scone for breakfast. But she was afraid that it would be too unhealthy. Melly was in conflict about this: As soon as she decided that she would eat a scone, she immediately thought of ten reasons why she shouldn't eat it. She tried to think about her Special Statement. She told herself to *Be rational!* but her fears were too strong— her anxiety was sky-high, and it wouldn't calm down. She had a hard time convincing herself to think rationally and logically.

"It was really hard. In a way, I was trying to be less rigid. I wanted a blueberry scone for breakfast. I love them. And blueberries are supposed to be really good for you. But then I got scared, like it would be too unhealthy. I thought I should have a bowl of plain oatmeal instead, like my mom does. I still worried about what my mom would think, even though I knew she wouldn't say anything. I couldn't decide what to do."

Melly's counselor encouraged her to do an experiment. She suggested this to Melly: "I know it will be hard, but eat a scone every morning for a week. Then write down your thoughts and feelings. A lot of your thoughts will probably be irrational, but that's okay. You're facing your fears, so we'd expect your anxiety and your irrational thoughts to increase. But stick with it. Use your Special Statement. Tell yourself, *Be rational!* And when you tell yourself to be rational, do some belly breathing—slow, deep breaths through your nose—and try to relax. See if your irrational thoughts lessen after a week. See if you can *teach yourself* to enjoy the scone."

Melly was scared, but she was courageous. She tried it. And it worked!

"It was hard. I ate one, and I felt okay, but then I got very anxious later. I had a lot of irrational thoughts and scary feelings, and I wrote them all down. I remembered to do some belly breathing. I reminded myself all day to *Be rational!* And I did calm down about it. I learned that a scone for breakfast didn't make me gain weight. It was so weird because I thought I had gained at least ten pounds that first day. But that wasn't possible or rational because after a few days, my jeans really did fit just fine. At the end of the week, I could eat a scone for breakfast and not totally freak out. I was still a little nervous, but I was okay. I was so proud of myself! I actually coped with my anxiety about the scone! I faced my fears, and I won!

"Now I look forward to breakfast. I have a scone every day. My mom helps: she buys me these scones from the bakery at our grocery store. I even got into making my own scones from a mix. They're delicious, and I have them with milk and juice. I'm full until lunch. I eat my scone slowly, so I can taste every bit! It's hard, but it's a relief. I mean, it's a nice treat in the morning. And my mom even tasted one of my scones and agreed that it's delicious! I sort of hate to admit it, but my mom liking the scone made me feel good!

Here's another routine that really helps Melly calm down and *Be rational!*

A Calming Chair

Melly has a rocking chair in her bedroom. She calls it her "calming chair." When she feels irrational thoughts bubbling up in her head about food, Melly sometimes goes to her room, closes the door, puts on some music, rocks in her chair, and repeats her Special Statement to herself.

"I really like my calming chair. I rock in it and say to myself, *Be rational! Be rational! Be rational!* I like having music on—I have a playlist for those times when I need to chill, and it helps. Usually it takes only a song or two, and I feel much better. I feel much more rational.

"You know, my life *is* better. I felt so much pressure to be such a perfect eater, but, really, it was such a waste of time and energy. It wasn't rational; it wasn't logical. Now I have more energy for my friends and for the piano—and that makes me much happier. I think I may always have a thing about eating healthily, but I'm a lot calmer about it now."

Special Statement:

"Size is just a number!"
—Tanya, age 17

T anya is an early developer. She got her period when she
was nine and has been wearing a bra since the summer
after third grade. Like many early developers, Tanya has
always been a little self-conscious about her body. But the
thing that makes Tanya the most self-conscious is the size of
her jeans. She was negatively perfectionistic about this issue:
she was totally unhappy with her appearance because she
thought she should be a smaller size, like her little sister or her
best friend.

"All I wanted to do was lose weight so I could fit into a
small size. I think a perfect size would be about two sizes
smaller than I am now. I still wouldn't be a size zero or even
close, but I think I would feel better about myself. I'd be like
everyone else. I could go shopping with my friends and not
feel huge and terrible. I just thought that I should be able to do
this. Actually, it's all I could think about. I couldn't even concentrate on my homework."

Tanya tormented herself with her negative perfectionism
about her body. She even sneaked into her sister's room one

day and tried on a pair of her jeans. Tanya was devastated because she couldn't even zip them up. She didn't console herself with the fact that her sister is only eleven and is a later developer than she was—her sister hasn't even hit puberty yet. Tanya couldn't stop thinking about the fact that the jeans didn't fit. She thought it was a sign that she was fat and ugly.

"I just couldn't stop putting myself down. I'd eat something, and then I'd think, *No, don't eat that. It will make your size even bigger. Put it down.* I said things like that to myself all the time."

Tanya thought that getting more exercise might help her get into smaller jeans. She thought of her aunt, who lives next door and power walks on the weekends. One Saturday morning Tanya asked to join her. She liked walking, and she liked spending time with her aunt. Now they walk together every week.

"I really like how I feel when I exercise, so that's good. But walking didn't make me any smaller. After a month, I still wore the same size. I was very frustrated. I was mad because I didn't reach my goal. But I did feel like my jeans fit better. I did feel like I was in better shape. But I didn't care. I just wanted to be a smaller size."

Tanya came up with her Special Statement on one of her walks with her aunt. Tanya shared her feelings: She talked about feeling bad about herself because she thought she "should" wear a smaller size. She felt bad because the size of her jeans was considered a "medium" instead of a "small."

Tanya's aunt listened for a while and then said, "Tanya, you have a beautiful figure. And you're a wonderful, kind person. Some of your friends still look like little girls, but you don't look like that anymore. And you're toned; you can keep up with me—and I'm pretty fast!" Tanya's aunt told her that *size is just a number* and that pretty soon her little sister will develop, and she'll wear a larger size, too.

"It was good talking to my aunt. What she said made sense. I decided to use *Size is just a number!* for my Special Statement. When I start getting down on myself, I think about that. I can even hear my aunt's voice tell me *Size is just a number* in my head. Is that weird? But I love her, and I don't think she'd lie to me. And my aunt wears larger size jeans than me, and I think she looks really good. She's active. She started taking a yoga class and taught me a pose. She even ran a half marathon— she's definitely not fat. So that means I'm not fat, either, and I guess my size is okay. At least I'm trying to think about it that way. My aunt told me to cut the size tags out of my jeans if the number bothers me so much, and I just might do that!"

Here's a sport that helps Tanya put her Special Statement into action—and use her perfectionism *positively*.

Kickboxing

anya volunteers at her church's Sunday school every week with two of her good friends. One Sunday, while they were all walking home, the girls decided to try a kickboxing class at the local YWCA. Tanya loved it! She never thought of herself as very athletic, but kickboxing makes her feel powerful! It helps channel her perfectionism in a positive direction.

"Now we go every Sunday, after church school. I feel cool when I kickbox.

"And I have a new goal for myself: I'm going to sign up for *real* boxing lessons! The best thing is that I'm more okay with not being so small. The size of my jeans is less important to me—I don't think about it as much. I try to think of my Special Statement and tell myself, *Size is just a number!* I try to think more about how I'm improving in class. I'm getting so much better at it. That makes me feel happier about myself. I'm happier with who I am, and I think I'm accepting my size better, too. For the first time in a long time I can see that my size isn't the worst thing in the world."

Getting the Picture

Maggie, Melly, and Tanya were all perfectionists who felt *imperfect*. Each girl focused her perfectionism negatively on her body image. Maggie wanted to lose weight and change the size of her nose so she could feel prettier; Melly felt comfortable eating only "healthy" food; Tanya felt self-conscious about her curves and put herself down because her jeans weren't the "perfect" size.

All the girls use their Special Statements to help them to stop obsessing about their negative points and to *stop being so hard on themselves.*

Maggie realized she had lots of positives in her life, and told herself to *STOP the negative; GO for the positive!* She also learned from her friend that being considered "perfectly pretty" isn't always a great thing. Maggie used her friend's concept—feeling pretty enough—to help keep her *going for the positive* and put her perfectionism on a positive track.

Melly had a lot of anxiety about food, and this led to irrational thoughts and behaviors that had a terrible effect on her body image. When she encouraged herself to think rationally and logically, she felt better. Melly's Special Statement *Be rational!* had a calming effect on her, as did rocking in her "calming chair." Melly learned through her rational experiment that she *could enjoy* her yummy, satisfying scone for breakfast. For Melly, it became the *perfect* way to start her day! (If you think you're as anxious as Melly was about food—or anything else—it would be a good idea to talk to a counselor or therapist, just as she did.)

Tanya's anxiety about her body fueled her negative perfectionism. She directed her perfectionism against herself because she didn't think the size of her jeans was "perfect"— until her aunt helped her realize that *Size is just a number,* and the number doesn't measure her attractiveness or her worth as a person. Tanya's Special Statement helped her let go of the negative, unrealistic dream of fitting into jeans that would never fit, and replace it with an *empowering goal*—taking real boxing lessons so that she'll be the best boxer she can be! She became positively perfectionistic about her new sport!

So if you're a perfectionist, and if your perfectionism makes you feel bad about yourself and your body, find a Special Statement that reminds you of the *positives* in *you!*

Perfectionism is a positive trait if you focus your energy in a positive direction.

Find goals that are good for your spirit.

Enjoy your drive to succeed.

Find pleasure in doing a good job.

And try to leave the self-criticism out of the picture, now and forever!

Sticks and Stones:

When You're Teased About Your Body

Has anyone ever teased you about being "fat"?

Has anyone ever made fun of you because you're naturally thinner than most girls?

Has anyone ever said that you have a body like a cartoon character?

Have you ever been teased about *any part* of your face or your body?

If your answer is "yes" to any of these questions, you're not alone. Studies have shown that 30 percent of middle school and high school kids are affected by teasing and bullying, and that a teen is teased every seven minutes! A recent National Crime Prevention Council survey shows that teasing and bullying is especially on the increase for teenage girls—and a *prime target for teasing* is a girl's physical appearance.

Any girl who's been teased about her looks will tell you two things:

1 The saying "Sticks and stones can break my bones, but names will never hurt me" is untrue—name-calling hurts *a lot.*

2 Being teased about your physical appearance is one of the most painful experiences *ever.*

Of course, boys tease girls. In fact, a boy may tease you because he likes you, and in a twisted way, he wants attention from you!

But all too often, the intention of teasing—especially about physical appearance—is mean-spirited. And worst of all, many girls are maliciously made fun of by *other girls.* Bystanders may not be so innocent; even nice girls may be afraid to speak up against the teaser. They may go along with the mean words and insults because they're afraid they'll be the next victim. After all, nobody's perfect—everyone has *something* they could be teased about. So the teasing continues. It's a sad, scary vicious cycle. Many girls are teased about how they look every single day.

At some schools, principals and teachers take teasing seriously. They've developed antiteasing and antibullying programs to raise awareness about the effects of teasing. These programs teach kids that bullies tease for many reasons, including the following:

❶ They may feel bad about themselves, so they try to make *others* feel bad about themselves.

❷ They may think that teasing will make them popular.

❸ They may have been teased themselves, so they think it's okay to tease other people.

Teachers hope that if students understand that ongoing teasing can lead to serious problems, they'll think twice before teasing others or going along with a bully, and as a result, school will be safer for everyone.

Unfortunately, every school in our country—or in the world!—doesn't have this kind of program. Too many girls who are teased have nowhere to turn, no one to talk to about their feelings, no one to help stop the teasing. If the teasing continues over a long period of time, a girl could become depressed, anxious, and develop a low self-esteem and poor body image.

If you're constantly being teased about your body, it's really important to get support. It's really important to walk away from the teaser with your head held high. It's really important to talk to someone about your feelings, so you can find ways to deal with the emotional effects of the teasing. It's really important to see that the problem is within the teaser, *not you.*

And it can be done! The taunts and rude remarks don't have to stick inside you and make you feel bad about yourself and your body.

You *can* learn to see that the problem has *nothing* to do with *your* appearance; it has *everything* to do with the insecurities within the person who is teasing you.

Here are the stories of three girls who've been teased about their bodies. They've all found ways to cope with the "sticks and stones" thrown their way by rude, insensitive people. Get some ideas from them. Let their strength and their resilience help *you* build up your own better body image.

 Special Statement:

"I'm beautiful, too."
–Elly, age 15

E lly is naturally very tall and thin. In fact she's taller and thinner than any other girl she knows. Elly has three sisters who are shorter than her and have normal weights. They don't understand how Elly can eat whatever she wants and never gain weight. Her oldest sister told her she's jealous, and some of Elly's friends are also jealous of her slimness.

"My sister says it's not fair that I can eat whatever I want and still be skinny. She said she has to watch her weight, but I think she looks great. I wish I had curves like her. I barely even need to wear a bra, and I'm a sophomore! And I have absolutely no hips. I feel like I look pathetic."

Elly has been teased about being skinny ever since she can remember. People say things like "Ewww—you're so skinny. You must be anorexic," or "You look like a twig. Is your mother Twiggy?" In seventh grade, one boy called her "Stringbean" and that became her middle school nickname— to this day, some boys still call her "Stringy." These comments make Elly feel very bad about herself.

"No one understands. They look at naturally skinny people in a negative way. I can't tell you how many times people I don't even know ask me if I'm anorexic. It makes me mad because I feel bad about being so skinny. But I can't help it, and I'm not doing anything wrong. I eat a lot, and people who don't eat lunch with me never see that. I eat a sandwich and chips and fruit and cookies. Sometimes I have fries with all that, or an ice cream sandwich. But people just assume I starve myself. It's like they discriminate against skinny people."

Elly has a hard time buying clothes—if the waist fits, the pants legs are too short; if the pants are the right length, they're falling off her slender body.

"One girl in my math class said in a really loud voice, 'Look at Elly. She's wearing capris in December.' I was so embarrassed. My jeans were way too short, but she didn't have to make such a big deal about it. Later that day I had swimming, and a girl pointed to me in the showers and screamed that I'm the skinniest person she ever saw. She said, 'You must be sick because your back bones show.' I was totally humiliated. I really felt like crying, but I didn't want to let anyone see how upset I was. I felt crushed inside. I felt totally alone, like no one could possibly understand."

That same day after school, just when Elly felt the worst, she read through a newspaper for a school assignment. An article on girls and body image caught her eye in the Health and Wellness section. It lifted her spirits—and gave her the idea for her Special Statement.

"There was this article about body image. Some high school girls designed a T-shirt that said, 'I Am Beautiful, No Matter What They Say.' I loved that! I get teased all the time for being skinny, but I *am* skinny, and so what? I want to feel like that's beautiful, too. Those girls had the right idea, and I use it for my Special Statement. My Special Statement is *I'm beautiful, too.* Every girl should be able to say that she's beautiful, no matter what—fat girls, skinny girls, everybody."

Elly says her Special Statement to herself every time she's

teased. She also says it first thing in the morning and the last thing at night. It's important for Elly to remind herself that when people tease her about being skinny, it doesn't mean that they're attractive and she's not. She, like everybody, has a right to feel beautiful, period! Elly thinks this helps boost her self-confidence—and her body image.

"When I remind myself that it's okay to think *I'm beautiful, too,* it helps. And even though I never met those girls who made the T-shirts, it helps to know that there are other girls out there who want to feel like they're beautiful, too, no matter what anyone else says. My mom says not to worry, that I'll fill out and have curves like all the rest of the girls. But until then, I just keep saying my Special Statement, and I feel a little better."

This is another way that Elly found to cope with the teasing—and reinforce that she's *beautiful, too*!

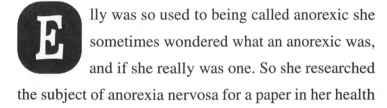

Action Plan

Fact-Finding

Elly was so used to being called anorexic she sometimes wondered what an anorexic was, and if she really was one. So she researched the subject of anorexia nervosa for a paper in her health class. The facts were reassuring: Elly found out that she is *not* anorexic. She learned that girls who have anorexia think they need to lose weight. They're obsessed with not eating, so they eat very, very little food. This information helped Elly feel more confident about herself.

Now when people tease her and call her anorexic, Elly silently says to herself, *I'm beautiful, too,* and tells them they don't know what they're talking about. She can make a strong argument in her own behalf. And even if they don't listen to her, Elly knows inside herself that she is right. She may be as thin as someone with anorexia, but her skinniness is natural and not due to an eating disorder.

"It's true, I am below normal weight for my height. But I've always been like this. My pediatrician said I've always been at the twenty-fifth percentile for weight and the seventy-fifth percentile for height. My dad was the same way. I must have his genes. My pediatrician said I'll gain weight eventually, probably when I'm twenty.

"Someone who has anorexia doesn't eat very much all day and exercises to burn calories and lose weight. She *wants* to lose weight! She never feels thin enough.

That is *so* not me! Burning up calories is the last thing on my mind. I'd be so happy if I could gain ten or even twenty pounds. That's how I know I'm not anorexic. And that's a big relief to me, because all that teasing was beginning to make me worry about it. I feel sorry for girls who are anorexic, but I'm not like that."

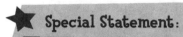

Special Statement:

"Miss Piggy is cute!"
—Faith, age 16

F aith is a cute girl. She is petite and has bright green eyes and a little turned-up nose. Faith has two older brothers who never tease her about how she looks. She is glad about this because one of her friends always complains that her older brother teases her nonstop. Faith also has a baby sister, whom she adores—her parents say she was the best "surprise" they ever had! Faith has lots of friends. She's a pom-pom girl, plays tennis, and is vice president of her school Pep Club.

But one thing in Faith's life isn't so great. A girl has teased her *constantly* about her appearance since the first day of high school. This has had a negative effect on Faith's body image: it made her feel ugly and embarrassed and helpless.

"It started out to be a joke. She said I had a pug nose and I looked like a pig. I told her she had a nose like a ski slope. We both laughed.

"But then she got mean. She kept calling me 'Miss Piggy' and made grunting noises when she saw me. I began to look at my nose and I think, *Maybe she's right. Maybe I do look like a pig.* That was so sad for me because I never used to have a problem with how I look. I felt really bad, and I couldn't do anything about it. I thought about getting a nose job. But I knew my parents wouldn't let me. But that's how bad I felt. It was hard to look at myself in the mirror because all I could see was how stupid my nose looked."

Faith asked her best guy friend if he thought she looked like a pig. He laughed and said, "No, you're really cute. Maybe that chick is jealous because all the guys think you're cute." Faith also asked the opinion of another good friend. The answer was the same: "She's probably jealous because nobody thinks she's cute, and everyone thinks you are." It felt good to get the support and feedback from her friends, and since their reactions were similar, Faith took their opinions to heart.

"That girl made me feel really insecure, but after I talked to my friends, I knew I had a choice to make. I could believe her and never have a good day again, or I could believe my friends who I trust. I don't trust that girl. All she does is make fun of me and my nose. And even if my friends weren't so complimentary—well, no one should tease anyone like that. It's just wrong.

"When I think about it, she's being ridiculous. What difference does it make—I mean, my nose is my nose! It's as though she's so focused on being mean to me—maybe she should think more about being a nice person, and then she'd have more friends."

One day when Faith was babysitting her little sister, she found her Special Statement. It was in—of all places—a Sesame Street movie!

"We were watching this old movie with Miss Piggy as the star. I decided that Miss Piggy is cute and really hilarious. I thought about the teasing, and I decided to make a joke out of it. So what if I look like Miss Piggy! She's so funny, and I laugh really hard at some of the things she says. I decided to take my being compared to Miss Piggy as a compliment! I decided to use *Miss Piggy is cute!* for my Special Statement.

"I know it might sound weird or crazy, but when I say to myself, *Miss Piggy is cute!* it makes the teasing all a joke. It makes me feel more powerful. Then I don't feel so embarrassed about my nose, and I don't worry as much about what people think or what that girl says. And since I don't get upset that much anymore, I think she's backing off. She didn't tease me about my nose yesterday or the day before. That's making progress!"

Here's a way that Faith puts her Special Statement into action—and puts the teasing into perspective.

Action Plan

Get Involved!

Faith is lucky because her math teacher is a sponsor for a group at school that raises awareness about bullying. And since Faith thinks that being teased about her nose was just like being bullied, she decided to join the group and try to make a difference.

"One day I told my math teacher about the teasing. She's cool, and I like her a lot. She told me to check out the group, and I did. Now I go every week. I didn't join the group because I need a lot of support anymore. I did for a while, and my friends helped with that. But I wanted to make a difference at our school. Some kids are teased so much for things they can't help: talking with a lisp, walking with crutches, being gay, or belonging to a different religion, such as Islam or Hinduism. Some of them don't have good friends. My experience made me see that being teased or bullied is so unfair, feels so bad, and needs to stop.

"Our group is cool. We do lots of stuff. We have picnics and car washes, to raise awareness. That's our main goal—to raise awareness at our school and our community so that things can change.

"One time a therapist came to speak to our group. She said that she was bullied when she was a teenager, and it left emotional scars. Now she works with kids who are bullied because she really does know how it feels. She said she was really impressed with our group and our goals. That was inspiring to everyone. It made us feel good about what we're trying to accomplish. It made me feel good about myself.

"I think everyone who is teased should have a Special Statement. Our group is going to talk about this next month, and maybe other kids will find Special Statements, too. I hope so because *Miss Piggy is cute!* works really well for me."

"I am fierce. I have resilience."

–Angelina, age 17

Angelina is a senior in a big public high school. She's an average student in most of her subjects, but she loves to draw and gets As in art. Angelina is an only child, and her parents are old enough to be her grandparents. She thinks there's a huge generation gap, even though they get along fairly well. She's shy with boys but has three really good girl-friends—girls she's known since first grade.

When Angelina was thirteen her grandmother died. They were very close, and Angelina felt sad and cried for weeks. She became depressed and anxious and developed a symptom of pulling out her hair, which is called trichotillomania. She's getting treatment for this problem and is doing much better. But Angelina still has to wear a wig to hide her very, very thin hair. In fact, she's practically bald. Because of this, she has been teased mercilessly for years by some very mean girls.

"I've never liked these girls. They've always been mean to me and my friends. When my friend's dog died when we were in sixth grade, they were even mean then. So when I lost my hair, they laughed and made fun of me. They've been teasing me for so many years. Last year one of them even yanked at my wig and tried to pull it off. That really hurt—it hurt my head and it hurt my feelings even more. What kind of a person would do that?

"It's hard enough for a normal teenage girl to feel good about her body and how she looks, but when you have a problem like mine, it's a thousand times harder. I want to feel pretty, just as every girl does. I don't want to have a problem with my hair, but I do. It's getting better: My hair is slowly growing, I'm taking medicine, and I'm learning better coping skills, so I don't pull it out so much. But I know I have a ways to go before I'm totally better. I just wish that these girls would leave me alone. They should put themselves in my shoes. They wouldn't like it if they had a problem with their hair and had people tease them about it."

Angelina's friends are great. They are all really supportive of her, and she is supportive of them. One day someone tripped Angelina in the hall and called her "baldy." She had to run to the washroom because she was crying—she was so embarrassed and upset. Her friend followed her and talked to her. She told Angelina, "You always bounce back." She said her mom told her that when a person bounces back after bad things happen, that means she has *resilience.* So that's how Angelina found her Special Statement.

"I've been through a lot. Not only losing my grandma, but also I've had this problem with pulling out my hair and the problem of girls teasing me. I've had a problem with depression and anxiety. But I'm getting through it. So I do have resilience, and that makes me feel better about myself. When I think about my resilience, I feel strong and determined. That's why my Special Statement is *I am fierce; I have resilience.* The 'I am fierce' part sort of makes me feel even stronger, like a lioness.

"I probably say my Special Statement ten times a day. I take a deep breath and say, *I am fierce; I have resilience,* to myself. I like having a Special Statement all my own. It helps me get through the hard parts of my day. I feel more positive after I say it, instead of negative and down on myself because I don't have a lot of pretty hair like the other girls. But I'm getting better. I think that having resilience and being fierce about it are very good qualities."

Here's another way Angelina puts her *fierce resilience* into action.

Action Plan

Wigs for Kids

Angelina thinks her experience with being teased about her hair makes her more sensitive to other kids who have problems. And she has a really cool goal. When her hair grows back, she wants to grow it past her shoulders, then cut it and donate it to kids who've lost their hair due to diseases like hers or cancer.

"I got this idea from my neighbor. She works for a group at a children's hospital.

"They do charity events at hair salons for kids with cancer. She said that one girl donated her hair and got all her friends to do it, too. I want to do that. I really want to help other people. That's a strong—*a fierce!*—feeling I have.

"So I asked my friends if they would do this, and my best friend, Geena, cut her hair and donated it in my honor! I promised myself that I'm going to donate my own hair, too. It's growing back now, slowly. I'm hoping that when I'm in college, I'll have hair to give to someone else. That would make me very happy—to help someone who's going through what I went through. That would be so cool! I think this shows that I really am *resilient*, because instead of feeling sorry for myself all the time, I want to bounce back and help someone else."

Here's another creative idea that helps Angelina fortify her fierceness and resilience.

Action Plan

Singing Solution

Angelina has a beautiful singing voice. She has always loved to sing. Angelina has been in her church's children's choir since second grade, and she is a soprano in her school's senior girls' choir. Singing has always brought peace of mind to Angelina. Like a muse, singing inspires her to have good feelings about herself.

"I love to sing. I love musical theater, and I love to sing songs from the shows. We saw *Wicked* last year and I bought the CD. I think I know every song.

"I sing in my room, sometimes with a CD, sometimes just by myself, a capella. I lose my insecurities when I sing. I love to sing "I'm Not That Girl" from *Wicked.* I don't know why—I just love that song. I lose myself in it. It's sort of weird, because it's a song about not feeling that beautiful, but I do feel beautiful when I sing it. Does that make sense? I guess it really expresses my feelings—like someone else feels the same way I do. And when I sing, it's one of the few times that I feel beautiful just the way I am. *Fierceness! Resilience!* I love those feelings!"

Getting the Picture

It's so hard to be the target of teasing, and all three girls were teased *big-time* about their physical appearance. And they all found Special Statements—and support—to help get them through these hard and hurtful experiences. And so can you!

Do people tease you about being too thin or too tall or too short or too big?

Elly had that experience. She knew the pain of being teased about something that she couldn't really change. Elly found that her Special Statement helped her remember that she has a right to say, and feel, *I'm beautiful, too,* in spite of what anyone else says. It's reassuring for Elly to know that other girls share her feelings—and even designed a T-shirt with a cool, good body-image slogan!

Elly's research for her health paper proved to her that her slenderness was due to being naturally thin—and not an illness like anorexia. Some girls have the opposite problem: they're naturally larger than average, not because they overeat, but because they are larger boned and more muscular. Whether you're naturally thin, like Elly, or naturally large—try to see this as a natural and special part of the picture of *you.*

Has anyone singled you out and made fun of a specific characteristic of your face? That's what happened to Faith. She was teased about her face—specifically, her nose. And this made her feel very bad about herself until she put the teasing in perspective and saw the ridiculousness of it. Her Special Statement, *Miss Piggy is cute!* helps her do this—it helps her turn the teasing into something benign and almost funny. Of course, the support from her friends was also a big help.

Do you have an emotional or physical problem that affects your appearance? Do people tease you about it? That's what happened to Angelina. She had trichotillomania, and she was teased by people who didn't understand or didn't care about her feelings. Angelina uses her Special Statement to remind herself daily that she is *fierce and that she has resilience—*

and that she bounces back from adversity. She also feels beautiful and resilient when she sings!

Angelina and Faith both discovered that the idea of helping others was very healing—it made them feel *good about themselves,* which is a good first step to good body image. It's so often true that our problems can have "silver linings" that show us the positives in our lives and in ourselves. Both girls' difficult experiences helped them gain the silver linings of empathy for others and the motivation to make a difference.

Like Angelina, lots of girls have problems that make them look a little different from the "average girl." For example, a person can be born with a cleft palate, which may make her talk with a lisp; a person can be born with webbed toes, which may always look a little "abnormal"; a person can have a serious illness like cancer that requires treatments that may make her gain or lose weight or lose her hair.

If you have a problem that affects your appearance and people tease you about it, don't hold your pain inside. Talk to your good friends. Join a group at school if you can. Talk to your parents. Talk to a therapist or counselor. Talk to your favorite teacher. Talk to the people in your life who love and support you. They can help you feel more secure and resilient in the face of obstacles to your self-esteem and body image.

Insensitive and mean people can make your life miserable if you give them the power to do so. Or they can be an unimportant nuisance, like a fly or a mosquito. The teasing stinks, but in the long run, it really *doesn't* matter what they think or say. The irony is that difficult experiences often make us strong and determined to succeed—sometimes even stronger and more determined than if we never had a problem in the first place!

So try out some of the things that help Elly and Faith and Angelina. See if any of them help you, too. Find a Special Statement, like they did, that helps you feel capable, grounded, resilient, and beautiful.

Having trouble thinking of a Special Statement? Maybe some of these ideas will help:

❶ On a blank piece of paper write, "I am unique because . . ." and then write anything that comes to mind— maybe you can even fill up the whole page.

❷ Integrity means honesty, sincerity, honorableness, and goodness. A person with integrity is a person who has principles by which she lives—she knows what is right and acts on it. On a blank piece of paper list the people who you think have integrity—family members, friends, teachers, political leaders, athletes, authors, or even celebrities. Think about how they've influenced your values and behaviors.

❸ Play a self-esteem boosting game with your best friend. Tell her what you admire about her. Then she tells you what she admires about you. Or vice versa—she can go first.

❹ Write down your favorite quote. (Here's a good one from the late author Mark Twain: "Keep away from people who try to belittle your ambitions. Small people always do that, but the really great make you feel that you, too, can become great.")

So surround yourself with *really great people* you trust. People whose opinions really do matter.

People who encourage and support you.

These people will help you see the real Beauty in You because they reflect your *goodness*.

They outshine the small people who tease you, any day.

Into My Mouth, onto My Hips:

When You're Honestly Overweight

Am I or am I not fat? This is the question that many girls repeatedly ask themselves.

And the answer may not be simple. A girl can *feel* like she is too heavy, but in reality her doctor says she is *healthy,* not too fat nor too thin. Or she can feel bloated before she gets her period and confuse this sensation with being "fat." Some girls constantly feel like they need to lose five or ten pounds and think when they do, their lives will magically be practically worry free! These are examples of girls who aren't really overweight or obese. Even though they may *feel* like they need to lose some weight, they're actually in a healthy weight range and, from a health perspective, should stay that way.

But sometimes a girl really *is* overweight. Some girls really *do* need to shed pounds, not to fit into a cultural ideal or to try to be a body type that nature didn't intend, but to ensure their good health. And luckily, if you are overweight, there are plenty of things you can do to increase your fitness and general well-being.

How do you know if you're overweight? The answer is not always clear-cut, but health professionals often use a measurement called a Body Mass Index, or BMI. This is basically a chart that gauges your weight in relation to your height. It is important to know that if you are very muscular, you may have a higher BMI yet still be at a healthy weight. If you would like to know what your BMI is, you can ask your doctor—he or she will probably have a chart to help you with this.

Some girls who are overweight don't see themselves as needing to lose weight. Sometimes it really doesn't seem to matter; an overweight girl may feel pretty, popular, smart, and generally satisfied with her life. She may think, "Why does my mom want me to lose weight? Why does my doctor tell me to exercise more? I'm happy just the way I am!"

But many times, a girl who is overweight feels secretly sad and self-conscious. She may wish she could wear the cute, trendy clothes that her friends wear, but these clothes may not look good on her or come in her size. She may wish she was more physically fit: she may tire easily and be unable to keep up with her friends in sports. She may be teased and suffer from stereotypes and prejudice. She may be called "stupid," "lazy," or "ignorant," even though these labels are far from the truth.

If you're unhappy about being overweight, you may have

tried to lose pounds and failed—many times! One reason for this may be that you're an emotional eater. This means that, even when you are not hungry, you eat to soothe your feelings.

You may also have major misconceptions about food. One important misconception is this: If a person wants to lose weight, she has to eat "low-fat" or "fat-free" everything, because eating fat is bad and will make her fat. And yet cutting out fat is *not* an effective way to lose weight. It *is possible* to eat too little fat! Nutritionists say that at least 20 percent of the calories most people eat need to come from fat, another 15 to 20 percent of daily calories need to come from protein, and the rest of the calories—usually around 60 percent—need to come from carbohydrates.

The fact is our bodies need fat to *function properly*. As Lynn Freedman, a nutritionist in the Chicago area and a specialist in treating patients with weight problems, says: "Cutting out fat is not the way to lose weight. Fat is much more important than people think. We need it for hormones, cell health, and brain functioning. We need it to feel that a meal is satisfying. It's a mistake to take fat out of the diet— it's as essential as protein and carbohydrates. Do we think that protein will turn us into protein? No—and that's about as logical as thinking that fat will make us fat. Every meal should have all the food groups in it, including a little fat—such as a teaspoon of olive oil, a tablespoon of peanut butter on toast, a few olives, or a few slices of avocado."

If you are overweight, you are not alone. Research shows that obesity, or extreme overweight, in teen girls doubled in the years between 1992 and 2002. In fact, recent statistics from the Centers for Disease Control tell us that around 17 percent of teens are overweight. That translates into *millions* of American girls who are exceeding their healthy weight ranges.

You may have tried everything to lose weight, without success. You may have tried exercising and "dieting," but the pounds just come back. But don't give up! There is plenty of hope!

You *can* learn the habits of healthy eating—and keep them for the rest of your life!

You *can* maintain a healthy weight for *you*!

You *can* achieve a better level of fitness and be in the best shape ever!

If you have any obesity-related health problems, like type 2 diabetes or high blood pressure, you *can* restore your health!

You *can* learn to deal with your emotions constructively instead of using food to soothe them.

You *can* feel proud of your body!

Read on and learn how three girls struggled with the pain of being overweight and emerged as body-image victors! See how their Special Statements help them feel happier and more content with their bodies. See how their new healthy habits have made them into *pictures of health*—and helped them to *picture* themselves as *perfect*!

And so can *you*! Absolutely!

Special Statement:

"Fit to be FREE!"
—Jesse, age 13

Jesse is in middle school at a small public school. She is looking forward to her bat mitzvah this year; she has been practicing hard for the big day. Jesse's family isn't very religious, but she wanted to have a bat mitzvah, the Jewish rite of passage into adulthood. Neither of Jesse's parents studied for this ceremony when they were young, but they support her decision. Jesse doesn't have many friends, but the two friends she does have are good, close friends. She wants to invite the whole seventh grade—all fifty of them!—to her bat mitzvah party. She hopes she can make some new friends that way.

Jesse has a weekend job grooming three horses at a local stable. She loves horses—her family used to own a horse, and her mom rode him in horse shows for a few years. Jesse likes to ride, too, although she's never been in a horse show. Still, she enjoys brushing the horses and feeding them treats, such as carrots and cut-up apples. Jesse feels she has a special relationship with the horses she takes care of. One of them nods his head every time she comes into the stable. Jesse feels that they love her just as much as she loves them.

Jesse is short for her age—she wishes she was at least five feet tall, but her mom is only four eleven. Her dad is not very tall, either, so she's not optimistic about this. Jesse is also heavy for her height. In fact, her pediatrician told her that she's around sixty pounds over her healthy weight. At first, this didn't faze Jesse. She was happy enough, was a good student, watched movies with friends on Saturday nights—life was good. And Jesse didn't know how in the world she could ever lose sixty pounds—it all seemed too overwhelming.

Then something happened last year that made Jesse think about losing weight. Her boss often let her exercise the horses at the stable, and one day a new horse came in as a boarder. It was very small, and Jesse thought he was so cute! She immediately wanted to ride him around the corral. But her boss was hesitant. She told Jesse, "I don't want to sound mean, but this horse is tiny, and he can't handle a lot of weight. I don't think it would be a good idea to ride him right now."

"I was so embarrassed. I never thought much about my weight. I mean, I knew I was too fat, but it never really mattered that much to me. My mom and dad are fat. My little brother is skinny, but he's only nine. So when my boss said that to me, I was, like, 'Wow. I do weigh a lot. I'm sorry. I'll try to lose some weight.' My boss was nice and told me not to worry about it, that I can ride all the other horses. But I felt really bad about my body for the first time. Now that I look back on it, it was a good thing in a way, but at the time I thought it was the worst, most embarrassing thing that ever happened to me."

Jesse found her Special Statement the next Saturday afternoon when she was working at the stable. As she brushed one of her horses in his stall, she decided to make a weight loss goal for herself. She didn't want to lose weight to be skinny; she just wanted to be *fit* and *free* to ride the new small horse. So her Special Statement became *Fit to be FREE!* In fact, she wanted to be able to do *anything* anyone else could do! She didn't want her weight to hold her back, ever again.

Jesse asked her boss how much weight she would need to lose to ride the small horse. The answer was around thirty pounds—which seemed more realistic than trying get down to the "healthy weight" her doctor suggested. She asked her doctor about it when she went in for a checkup, and the reply was: "Great! Start with thirty pounds and see how you feel."

Jesse had no idea how to lose weight. She never paid any attention to what she ate. She never thought about whether she was eating healthy food or junk food. She was totally uninformed about healthy eating habits, and she didn't exercise very often, except for riding on the weekends.

Fortunately, Jesse's doctor was also a registered dietician. She told Jesse that if she ate healthier and exercised a little more, she would probably lose some weight without much of a problem. She gave Jesse these tips:

1. Try to get twenty to thirty minutes of exercise every day—fast walking is a good place to start.

2. Cut down on fried fast food—try Subway sandwiches and salads instead.

3. Try to eat grains at meals—this can help keep snacks healthier. A handful of peanuts or almonds and/or a cup of yogurt with fruit are healthy, filling snacks.

4. Eat one treat at a time—don't load up on junk food. Pudding and frozen yogurt are good treats because they have some nutritional value: calcium.

5. Drink more water and less soda, including diet soda.

The doctor's tips helped Jesse translate *Fit to be FREE!* into action. Here's how she does this.

Action Plan

A Good, Old-Fashioned Walk

Jesse took her doctor's advice about exercise. She made time to walk around her neighborhood for thirty minutes after she got home from school most days. She actually found that this was a good way to unwind after being cooped up in the classroom all day. It was, literally, like a breath of fresh air, and it gave her energy!

"I used to come home from school and feel exhausted. But walking helps me get my stress out. I come home after I walk, and I feel much better. I'm in a better mood."

Here's another way Jesse reinforces her Special Statement.

Smarter Lunch Choices

For school lunches, Jesse used to fill up on hot dogs and fries. But now she brings a healthy lunch—either a turkey sandwich or a peanut butter and jelly sandwich, fruit, yogurt, and, yes, a cookie!

"My doctor said I could have one treat at a time. She said that means I can have a cookie, but not a cookie and fries—if I have a cookie, the other stuff should be healthy. So my treat for lunch is a cookie. That way no one will think I'm weird, like on some crazy diet. They'll see I'm eating normally and healthier, and that's okay. Other girls eat healthy foods at lunch, so I won't be the only one. And really, sometimes I'm not even hungry for the cookie, so I just eat half or give it to my friend. My doctor said that means I'm getting more in touch with my hunger, and she said that's very good because I didn't used to know if I was hungry or not."

But soon Jesse realized that losing weight was not going to be easy. It was hard for her to cut down on fried fast food because she was used to eating it almost every day. Even though her lunches were healthier, Jesse and her best friend always stopped for fries on the way home from school. Her mom stopped for fast food several times a week for dinner when she worked late. For dinners, Jesse loved burgers and fries and, best of all, a big chocolate milkshake! Her doctor told her she could have those things once in a while, maybe once a week, but that she should try to skip fried fast food as a rule.

The doctor also told Jesse and her mom that family support is important when one family member is trying to eat healthier. She told them that it would be really good if there were healthier choices for meals and snacks at home. Jesse and her mom talked about this issue. Her mom admitted that everyone in the family could probably benefit from eating healthier, so it would be a great idea to have healthier food choices in the fridge. Her mom suggested they could get deli sandwiches instead of burgers when she had to bring home dinner—Jesse's dad likes them better than burgers, anyway.

Here's another way Jesse's family helps support *Fit to be FREE!*

Hearty Soup, Healthy Supper

Jesse's mom thought of a healthy meal that would be fun for her and Jesse to cook together. She suggested that they make a big pot of soup and freeze portions for the microwave.

Jesse loved the idea, so that's what they did! They made lentil soup with chicken sausage (a healthier choice than ham or pork sausage); turkey and vegetable soup with lots of veggies, including carrots, celery, and onions; and chicken noodle soup. They bought some bags of premade salad so Jesse could fix one for herself if she had to eat alone. The new dinners were healthy, but most important, they were delicious!

"I'm so glad my mom helped me with this. We don't sit down for meals as a family very much, but it does help to have healthy food around. Sometimes I do crave fries, and I won't lie, I still eat them sometimes. But I really like the soup and sandwich and salad idea for dinner. I have a big bowl of soup, so I don't feel like I'm depriving myself. I usually have a sandwich, too—sometimes it's just half a sandwich—and a salad. Now I feel like I'm going to reach my goal and not feel hungry. That's what I was afraid of if I went on a diet—that I would feel hungry. But this isn't really a diet. It's just substituting healthy food for fast food. My mom and my whole family have been supportive, so that helps. My friend and I are getting bagels instead of fries after school. That helps, too!

"It is not easy. I'm trying to change my habits and I'm not perfect. But I am losing weight. I am on my way to feeling *Fit to be FREE!* My doctor told me not to weigh myself at home; she would weigh me once a month in her office. She said people get obsessed with their weight if they weigh themselves too much. She said that could lead to weird behavior with food."

After almost a year, Jesse reached her goal, minus five pounds. Her biggest reward was getting on that little horse and riding him around the corral!

"I'll never forget how cool I felt. I felt so proud of myself and good about my body. It took me a long time, but I did reach my goal. *Fit to be FREE!* is a great Special Statement for me. It's a good thing to keep telling myself. My doctor said I'm much more physically fit and healthier than I was last year. I'm going to keep up my routine. I'm going to keep exercising—I'm on the swim team—I'm going to keep eating healthily, and if I lose more weight, that's fine. But if I don't, I honestly don't care.

"I feel like my Special Statement helps me remember that being healthy and fit means that I'll be able to be free to do whatever I want to do. I feel so much better about my body now. I really am *Fit to be FREE!*"

Special Statement:

"Healthy feels happy."
—Denise, age 17

Denise goes to a big public high school and is one of the most popular girls in her junior class. She has tons of friends, both boys and girls. She is vice president of the student council. She is practically a straight-A student. She has had several poems and photographs published in her school newspaper, where she is an editor.

The only glitch in Denise's life is that she's extremely overweight.

Denise's mom is also overweight, but she doesn't seem to care. She told Denise that she is proud of her body and that Denise's father loves her just the way she is—he wouldn't want her to lose a pound! Denise's brother, two years older, thinks that too many girls in her high school are too skinny. Denise's size has never been an issue for her friends or her family. If anything, they've all accepted her for who she is, extra pounds and all. Still, Denise has never felt very happy about her body.

"No one ever said anything to me about losing weight. The women in my family are all overweight. It's sort of normal. My weight is mostly in my legs and butt, and that's not considered a bad thing in my family.

"I just really like to eat. I got into the habit of eating doughnuts at night when I do homework. I didn't think I could ever stop—it was such a routine, and it helped me stay up and do my work. I knew it probably wasn't the best thing. I was so much heavier than all my friends, but I guess I just accepted that I'd never be thin."

In the summer after her sophomore year, Denise signed up to go on a community service trip with some of her friends from school. It sounded like a cool trip—she'd help build houses in the Appalachian Mountains and would get to tutor economically disadvantaged children in math and English. This really appealed to Denise because she wants to be a teacher someday.

"I looked forward to that trip for years. You had to be at

least sixteen to go. I was so excited that I was finally going."

Denise had to have a physical exam for the trip, so her mom arranged an appointment with her doctor. It was a thorough examination—Denise had to go in beforehand for some lab work. After the exam, the doctor told Denise that she was generally healthy. She could go on the trip, no problem. But there were a few potential problems. Denise's HDL, or good cholesterol, was low, and her LDL, or bad cholesterol, was in the moderate to high range. Her blood pressure was also on the high side of normal and had crept up a lot since the previous year. Denise's doctor was concerned that she was at risk for cardiovascular problems, and the probable cause was her weight.

The doctor asked Denise's mom if hypertension or type 2 diabetes runs in their family. Denise's mom replied yes to both. Then the pediatrician asked if obesity runs in the family. Again, the answer was yes.

"My doctor said that these diseases—cardiovascular problems and diabetes—could be related to the obesity. She said that I should try to lose some weight for health reasons, because the longer I was overweight, the harder it would be to lose weight, and the more at risk I'd be for bad health.

"To be honest, I felt scared but kind of relieved. Someone was actually telling me to lose weight. And my mom listened, too. Her sister had died of a stroke a few months before. She wasn't very old—I think in her forties. My mom also has high blood pressure and type 2 diabetes. She told my doctor, 'I've been thinking about losing weight myself ever since my sister died.' Then she said to me, 'Let's try to be healthier. We can try together.'

"All of a sudden I felt so sad. I don't know why. Maybe it was about my aunt. Maybe I was scared my mom would die. Maybe I was sad because I was so big. So I agreed with my mom. I wasn't that worried about myself, but I was worried about her. I told her I'd try to be healthier with her. I was so emotional—I almost cried in my doctor's office!"

The next day, Denise thought of her Special Statement.

"I thought about how I almost cried in front of my doctor. I didn't want to be sad like that anymore. I didn't want to worry about my mom. I wanted both of us to be healthy, and I wanted to be happy, so this came to my mind: *Healthy feels happy*. So that's my Special Statement now."

Denise and her mom needed professional advice to lose weight, so their doctor referred them to a nutritionist who specializes in treating overweight patients. The nutritionist was very supportive and understanding—she had been 100 pounds overweight when she was in college. She really knew what it felt like to be faced with the task of losing lots of weight.

But the nutritionist was also very clear. She told them, "You don't need a diet. You need some healthy eating and exercising habits. You need to use good self-care skills. You need to develop new lifelong healthy-living plans. We're not going to focus on pounds; we're going to focus on being fit and being well. That's the key to weight-loss success, and I'll help you with it."

Denise and her mom had some wrong ideas about how to lose weight and be healthy. For example, Denise thought that it was bad to eat fat. Her mom thought that eating food with cholesterol raises cholesterol. Both Denise and her mom thought they'd never be able to eat sugar ever again.

The nutritionist gave Denise and her mom some helpful information that corrected their misconceptions. She told them that essential fatty acids—often labeled as "fat"—are important for our bodies. Denise and her mom learned that certain fats, sometimes called mono fats, are particularly good for the body. They are found in nuts and nut butters, such as peanut butter and cashew butter, avocados, olives, and olive oil.

The nutritionist also shared a surprising fact: Mayonnaise isn't a bad thing to use on a sandwich because it contains mostly vegetable oil and a little egg. If they enjoyed mayonnaise, they could have some! Denise was very happy about this because she couldn't imagine a turkey sandwich without a little mayonnaise.

The nutritionist told them that saturated fats and trans fats are the fats to avoid or cut down on because they're bad for heart health. Saturated fats are found in fatty meats, fried foods, cream, butter, and whole milk. Trans fats can be found in snacks, such as chips, candy, or any food using partially hydrogenated plant oils.

Also, sugar does not have to be totally avoided, but it's best to limit sweets because sugar doesn't have any nutritional value—it's like eating extra calories but getting no nutrition.

Denise learned things she never knew from the nutritionist, and she's putting the new knowledge to work. She uses it to fuel her resolve to live by her Special Statement—to be *healthy* and feel *happy.* Here's how she does this.

Action Plan

The Antidiet, Just Darn Good Food Plan:

Denise and her mom are trying to eat according to the nutritionist's suggestions. Denise made up a name for their new habits: The "antidiet, just darn good food plan," and it is! This plan goes something like this:

For breakfast, Denise has two slices of peanut butter

toast, fruit, and milk. Her mom has two eggs and a piece of whole grain toast, fruit, and coffee.

For lunch they have sandwiches: turkey or chicken with a little mayonnaise, lettuce, and tomato; or tuna salad with lettuce and tomato; plus fruit and yogurt, then something to drink (Denise loves skimmed milk, her mom has water).

For an after-school snack, Denise substitutes baby carrots and a scoop of hummus (a delicious chickpea spread) for chips. Or sometimes she has pudding and fruit—blueberries or strawberries—or a handful of almonds if she's in a hurry.

Dinners are typically chicken or lean meat, vegetables, a big salad, and a serving of rice or a potato, with a dessert of fruit salad topped with yogurt. Denise learned to like whole grain products like brown rice, which is more nutritious than white rice. She also learned that she loves baked sweet potatoes, which is good because they have more nutrition than white potatoes.

"I used to hate brown rice, but now I think it has a nice, nutty flavor. I like whole wheat bread now, too, and I never tasted that until recently. It took some getting used to, but I prefer it now."

And last but not least, the treats. Denise's treat is one blueberry muffin and a cup of chamomile tea with honey, which she eats when she does homework at night—a healthy variation of her former unhealthy doughnut habit!

"It really isn't a diet, so to speak. It is about making healthier choices—but most of all it is an education. I didn't understand much about healthy eating before we saw the nutritionist. Now when I eat something that's not so great, like a piece of cake, I know I can make up for it by eating healthy foods the rest of the day. One piece of cake doesn't mean that I have to eat five pieces. I didn't want to choose doughnuts for my treat because I was afraid I'd get out of control. But a muffin is fine."

Here's another way Denise puts *Healthy feels happy* into action.

Action Plan

On the Move!

 Denise used to be a fairly inactive person. She preferred reading to playing sports, doing art to doing push-ups, and she never walked to school, even though it was only a half mile from home. But this has changed. Now, Denise is making an effort to be more active.

"My nutritionist told me, 'You don't have to do hard, sweaty exercise if you hate it. But you do have to move your body more.' So I'm a 'mover' now! I walk home from school unless it's really bad weather, I found a yoga class at the Y that I like, and I walk stairs instead of using elevators and escalators. Maybe I'll work out on the machines at the Y someday, but for now, I'm just trying to move my body more. And I think it helps. I do feel healthier and *happier* after I've gotten a little exercise."

After a month, Denise and her mom went back to the nutritionist to be weighed. They were both happy and proud of themselves—Denise had lost four pounds and her mom had lost three!

Denise realized that she felt a lot better, even though her weight loss was just getting started. Exercise was beginning to give her definition in her legs, and this made her feel stronger. Her healthy eating habits were giving her more energy. And all that made Denise feel *happy* about being *healthy*.

"Now I'm happy because my mom and I are both

getting healthy. I'm losing weight, and it feels great. My Special Statement sounds so simple but it works for me. *Healthy feels happy* is so true!"

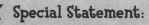

Special Statement:

"What am I really feeling?"
–Stacie, age 15

Stacie recently moved with her family from a small town in upstate New York to a big city in Illinois. At her old school, she had lots of friends and was an honors student. At her new school, she hasn't met many friends and is an average student. At her old school, Stacie played the flute in the marching band. At her new school, there are too many flutes, so she was asked to play the clarinet. Stacie didn't want to do that, so now she doesn't have any extracurricular activities. In general, Stacie feels miserable at her new school.

"I didn't want to move, but my dad got a job in Chicago, so we had to move. My little sister is in fourth grade, so it didn't matter that much to her. She's outgoing and already has a ton of friends. But it's harder for me. I'm more of an introvert. I had lots of friends in New York. I had known them since kindergarten, and I was so comfortable there. I'm not comfortable here. The girls wear expensive jeans and cool clothes that I can't wear because I'm not thin. I feel like I'll never find friends, never fit in."

Around six months after she moved, Stacie got a really bad sore throat and had to go to the doctor. Her new doctor—which was also uncomfortable because she had gone to the same doctor in New York for fourteen years—examined her and gave her some medicine. Then he asked Stacie some good questions. He asked her if she had any problems sleeping. Stacie answered, "Yeah, sometimes I can't get to sleep." Then the doctor told her she looked a little sad and asked if she ever felt like crying. Stacie said, "Yes, all the time since we moved." The doctor asked Stacie what she did when she felt sad. Stacie thought a minute and said, "I eat cookies and ice cream."

Stacie's doctor said he understood and that lots of people use food for comfort. But Stacie's weight, which had always been a little above average, had grown to be in the high range for her height—she'd gained thirty pounds since the move. Her doctor said it would be good to eat healthier and to find better ways to deal with her emotions, so she'd stop gaining weight and begin feeling better.

"I knew the doctor was right. I have a weird relationship with food. I love it, and I hate it. It was there for me when I came home from school and felt bad. It was there late at night when I didn't want to do my homework. It was always there for me—I didn't feel bad when I ate. I really didn't feel anything. But I ate so much I got a stomachache, then I hated myself.

Stacie's doctor told her mom that he was concerned about Stacie using food to cope with her feelings. He gave her a card with the name of a therapist who specializes in overeaters. One day, after Stacie had forgotten about the conversation with her doctor, her mom told her she had an appointment with the therapist. Stacie was more than a little upset.

"I didn't really see why I had to talk to a therapist. I wasn't happy, but there was a definite reason: I missed my old school and my old friends. Who wouldn't be unhappy? I didn't think that this was abnormal. I didn't like being fat, but I honestly didn't really care that much. I thought, *I'll lose weight when I'm ready.*"

Stacie agreed to meet the therapist once to see if it would help her feel better. She was pleasantly surprised.

"The therapist was nice, and she was really concerned about how I was feeling. We didn't even talk that much about my weight, except that I told her my doctor said that I was too fat and should eat better. She told me we'd work on that, but first she wanted to get to know me. I agreed to go back and talk to her."

In therapy, Stacie learned that she had some symptoms of depression: the problems with sleep, her sadness, and her overeating all indicated she was depressed. The therapist thought that her sad, depressed feelings were probably caused by the loss of her old friends and familiar surroundings. She thought that as Stacie learned more positive ways to deal with her feelings, her sadness might lift, and she might not need to use food to comfort herself. If this didn't work, Stacie might need antidepressant medicine. But learning how to deal with her feelings did work! Plus, as she began to examine her feelings, Stacie discovered her Special Statement.

"I don't mind going to therapy too much now. I don't feel so depressed. I'm learning some good things. My therapist told me to keep a 'food and feelings journal.' I did. I wrote down what I ate on one side of the paper and my feelings on the other. Then I brought it to therapy, and we looked at it together.

"I found out that when I eat a lot of junk, I'm usually not hungry. I'm sad and sometimes tense and angry. I also realized that eating doesn't really help these feelings. It just makes things worse: I get mad at myself, and then I just eat more."

Like many girls, Stacie has a hard time identifying her feelings; she doesn't always *know* how she feels. She wanted to find a Special Statement that would help her with this.

"I thought to myself, over and over, *What am I really feeling?*

Then I decided to make that my Special Statement—well, it's really more like a Special Question. But I think it's a good one for me. When I know how I feel, at least I know that I'm not hungry and that food is not the answer to dealing with the feeling.

Stacie's therapist suggested a tool to help her answer her "Special Question." Here it is.

Action Plan

A Feeling List

Stacie and her therapist made up a list of possible feelings. When Stacie asks herself, *What am I really feeling?* she looks at the list and tries to label her feelings. Sometimes she thinks of a feeling that's not on the list, then she adds it for future reference.

Here's Stacie's feelings list so far:

Angry	Scattered	Content
Confused	Hyper	Strong
Frightened	Anxious	Heavy-headed
Irritable	Happy	Inspired
Jittery	Pathetic	Crazed
Goofy	Joyful	Empty

Relaxed	Numb	Annoyed
Grateful	Supersensitive	Sad
Bored	Spacey	Defeated
Pretty	Worried	Deflated, like a
Passionate	Tense	popped bal-
Connected	Prickly	loon
Excited	Crawling out of	Lonely
Stupid	my skin	Down in the
Shy	Afraid	dumps
Insecure	Panicked	Overwhelmed
Distracted		

"I ask myself *What am I really feeling?* and then I use my feeling list to figure it out. When I can see how I feel, it's easier not to eat. It's easier to see that I should find something else to do to calm down."

Yet labeling feelings is one thing; calming them down is another. And there were lots of times when Stacie couldn't figure out how to *calm down* her feelings. She needed to take her Special Question, *What am I really feeling?* to a more active level. So her therapist helped her make a new list. Here it is.

Replacement Behaviors List

tacie's replacement behaviors list helps her find things she can do besides eat to calm down and cope with her feelings. Stacie is constantly thinking of new things to add to the list.

Here are some examples from Stacie's replacement behaviors list:

❀ Take a shower—for sad feelings

❀ Brush my teeth—for anxious and worried feelings

❀ Walk around the block—for irritable feelings

❀ Call a friend from my old school in New York— for lonely feelings

❀ Pet my cat—for sad, lonely, and empty feelings

❀ Listen to rock music—for happy feelings

❀ Pop the bubbles in bubble wrap—for jittery feelings

❀ Play my flute or piano—for down-in-the-dumps feelings

❀ Do ten push-ups—for tense and angry feelings

❀ Stand facing the wall and push really hard for thirty
seconds with both hands—for tense and angry feelings

❀ Close the door to my room and scream—for crawling
out of my skin feelings

❀ Belly breathing—for scattered feelings

"My Special Question helps me to know what my feelings are. I ask myself, *What am I really feeling?* a lot. I love lists, so the feelings list helps. Then when I know my feelings, I use my other list. I pick a behavior besides eating to deal with them. This doesn't work one hundred percent of the time, but every time it does work it gets a little easier not to cope with my feelings with food. When it doesn't work, my therapist said not to judge myself. Just try to get back on track the next time.

"I'm trying to slow down and enjoy food. I read somewhere that when you focus on tasting and enjoying your food, it's like meditation. I never used to smell food or taste it. I just ate it—fast. But now that I'm dealing with my feelings better, I think I'm enjoying my food better, too.

"And the feelings don't stay that long. They never stay more than a day, and usually not even that long—sometimes just a few minutes, sometimes an hour.

"So when I ask myself, *What am I really feeling?* I also ask myself, *Why should I eat to numb my feelings?* That behavior could stay with me forever.' I'm also thinking of joining an overeaters anonymous support group for teens that my therapist told me about. I used to hate groups, but now I'm sort of interested in talking to people who are going through what I'm going through. At least I'm willing to give it a try.

"I feel like I have more control now, and I feel happier at school, too. I have a little more confidence, and I've made a few friends. I haven't lost a lot of weight, but I haven't gained any, either. Really, I am a lot happier."

Getting the Picture

Jesse, Denise, and Stacie all had problems with their weight, which led to problems with body image. Jesse's weight prevented her from riding the small horse at the stable; Denise was on the verge of developing health problems because of her weight; and Stacie gained weight because she used food to cope with her feelings. All three girls had negative feelings about their bodies, and they all found ways to eat healthier and feel better.

Do you lack the *information* you need to be a healthy eater? Jesse and Denise did! Neither girl had correct knowledge about nutrition or food groups; they didn't really know much about healthy eating habits. They didn't know that to lose weight, you have to eat from all the food groups, and that you have to eat regularly and not let yourself get too hungry! Regular exercise is also important. When Jesse and Denise were able to get more exercise and eat healthy meals and snacks—which included treats!—they were able to lose weight and feel better. Their Special Statements help keep them on track. Jesse reminds herself she wants to be *Fit to be FREE!* and Denise tells herself that *Healthy feels happy.*

Like Stacie, do you use food to cope with your feelings? Many times girls who use food as a coping skill feel depressed and anxious. You may feel disconnected from your body: you may not really be in touch with being hungry or full. You may not think about whether or not you're feeding your body too much. The goal of eating may be to reach a "numb" feeling rather than to nourish your body.

If you use food as a coping skill, try to label your feelings and find actions, other than eating, that will soothe them. Use Stacie's feelings list and her list of replacement behaviors to help you identify *your own* feelings and replacement behaviors.

It may also help to find a therapist who has experience with overeaters, like Stacie did. That way you can have some expert advice and support as you try to find more positive ways to deal with your feelings. (It's especially important to find a therapist if you've felt depressed or anxious for more than a couple of weeks.) In time, food will become what it's supposed to be: a delicious means of nourishing and nurturing yourself and your body. Eventually you'll feel more connected to your body and your appetite; they will feel more like a part of yourself.

So go for it!

Go for health!

Go for energy!

Take off pounds and take on a brand new positive picture of yourself.

You are totally worth it!

8

A Pretty Picture:

I Am Already Perfectly Me

Body image is such a complicated topic, as the girls' stories have shown.

- ❀ Body image can be distorted. We often see ourselves differently—and more negatively—than others see us.
- ❀ Body image can be affected by our worries about food and weight.
- ❀ Body image can plummet when we compare ourselves with other girls or especially celebrities.
- ❀ We may wish for a different body shape and bone structure.
- ❀ We may wish that we were the only person in the universe to have no "flaws."
- ❀ Body image may be affected by the insensitivity of others, and the teasing that can go along with this.
- ❀ Body image may be affected by being overweight and not knowing how to be healthy.

❋ Body image can be affected by the media, our
   moods, our relationships with our friends and
   families, and where we live.

The list of things that can affect body image goes on and on
and on!

And yet of all the many issues that affect body image, current studies show that one of the most important issues is our
self-esteem, or how we value (or don't value) ourselves.

In fact, Dove's recent global research project, "Beyond
Stereotypes: Rebuilding the Foundation of Beauty Belief,"
shows that when a girl feels good about herself and has good
self-esteem, she's more likely to see herself as confident,
smart, energetic, and beautiful. Conversely, when a girl feels
bad about herself and has low self-esteem, she's more likely to
see herself as worthless, insecure, stupid, and ugly. This study
also points out that when girls feel bad about their bodies,
they're more likely to avoid normal daily activities, such as
voicing their opinion, going to a party, shopping for clothes,
or even going to school.

When you have a low opinion of your body, negative
thoughts can spin round and round. You may ask, "If I can't
feel good about my body, how can I ever really feel good

about myself?" or "How can I value myself when I wish I were taller or shorter or thinner or curvier?" or "How can I like myself when I hate my tummy? How can I feel confident when my acne is terrible? With all my insecurities, how in the world will I ever see a pretty picture of me?"

True, it's not easy to interrupt the negative things we say to ourselves. We're so used to putting ourselves down! We're so used to viewing media images that make us feel inferior! We're so used to thinking that our appearance must fit a certain mold that friends, family, or society make for us! We're so used to seeing ourselves as so . . . imperfect!

And yet, according to the Dove study, and countless others, most girls agree that standards of beauty should be broader. Most girls agree that in our ethnically and racially diverse country—and world—beauty comes in different colors, shapes, and sizes. Most girls agree that they should be more supportive of one another's beauty. And so there is hope!

It takes practice, but we *can* feel beautiful.

We *can* feel full of value.

We *can* feel *picture perfect* just the way we are!

Dorothy in *The Wizard of Oz* had her Special Statement, "There's no place like home." It's not uncommon for musicians, athletes, actors, dancers, singers, and public speakers to say Special Statements to themselves for confidence and

inspiration. Like them, you can discover a Special Statement
that *inspires* you and makes you feel *more confident* about
your body and yourself.

So find a Special Statement that has *special meaning* to you.
Find one that reflects how you want to live your life. Having
trouble thinking of one? Think of quotes from books, or lyrics
to songs, or something you overheard somewhere. Think of an
adult, such as a parent or a grandparent or a teacher, whom you
admire. What are her or his favorite sayings? Or check the
Resources in the back of this book for more ideas.

Once you've found your Special Statement, say it over and
over to yourself. Say it to yourself when you wake up in the
morning. Repeat it again when you go to bed.

Repeat it to yourself whenever you feel insecure about your
body, or whenever you feel any negative thoughts about yourself brewing inside your head. The more times you think of
your Special Statement, the less room you'll have for the
negative thoughts. Your brain will have more space for your
positive, good self-esteem thoughts—thoughts that will help
you feel better about yourself and your body.

And with practice—after you've used your Special
Statement lots of times—you'll feel like it is part of you. It
will help keep you positive. It will help raise your self-esteem.
It will help keep you focused on your goal of good body

image, good energy, confidence, and success.

Don't forget, you can change your Special Statement any time, anywhere. If you've used yours for a while and find yourself drawn to a different one, make a change. Or use both of them—or think of even more! You can collect Special Statements to go along with your different feelings and moods and situations. One Special Statement could lift you up when you feel down, and another could support you when you feel secure and confident.

All feelings are temporary—they're constantly changing, constantly going up and down, like the horses on a merry-go-round. Bad body-image feelings, like any other feelings, are temporary, too. They're like dust on the picture of a beautiful you—they mar your vision; they make your beauty hazy and unclear. It's not so easy to just blow off the dust, but *there are ways* to increase your self-esteem, so you can see your own special beauty.

Your Special Statement is one way. It will help you give yourself clear, positive messages.

Regular exercise is another way. Doing something active every day helps us feel better about our bodies and feel happier and less stressed from the inside out.

Relaxation—including getting enough sleep—is important, too. It's hard to feel happy and good about ourselves when we're exhausted and depleted from a lack of rest. Yoga, meditating, chilling with friends, massaging the back of your neck, reading a good book, knitting a scarf: these are some ways many girls fit a little relaxation into their busy lives.

And communication—connection with others—is another great antidote for bad body-image feelings. Connecting with others can be *soothing*; sharing your feelings with people who really understand can *comfort* you. It can make you feel more *confident* when you know that there are people in this world who can "put themselves in your shoes" and appreciate you just the way you are. Connecting with others can help us see our good points and minimize the things we wish were different about ourselves. And when we can see our good points, we get a glimmer of the beauty in ourselves. We start to imagine ourselves in a prettier picture.

So talk with your friends. Talk to your mom, or another trusted woman; your relationship with the women in your life can have a positive effect on your body image.

Does your school have a body-image support group for girls? Many high schools have them—and they're a great way to make new connections. When a girl meets other girls who want to feel better about their bodies, she often feels instantly connected. It's easy to support—and accept support from—like-minded girls. If your school doesn't have a body-image support group, go to your counselor and find out how to start one! Chances are it will fill up very quickly!

Surround yourself with good body-image friends—friends who don't dwell on the downfalls of their bodies but instead try to feel happy in their own skins. When we hang out with people who have a basically healthy attitude about themselves and their bodies, well, the feeing can be contagious! All of a sudden we start to feel happier about ourselves and our bodies, too!

And have fun with beauty! Instead of punishing yourself with diets and self-doubt, treat yourself to something *divine.* Women have used beauty rituals for thousands of years to feel pretty, inside and out.

So invite your friends over and give one another foot massages and pedicures.

Put a deep conditioner on your hair and wrap it up in a warm towel for a half hour.

Take a relaxing bubble bath.

Highlight your best facial feature with a little makeup or a new haircut.

Lie on your back in bed and stretch all your limbs when you wake up in the morning.

Take time to do something special for yourself and your body every day. Little body-caring, beauty treats can lift our spirits and help us enjoy, and draw attention to, our natural attractiveness.

And the more we can enjoy our natural attractiveness, the better we feel about ourselves.

And the better we feel about ourselves, the better we feel about our bodies.

And the better we feel about our bodies, the easier it is to feel *picture perfect* just the way we are!

Afterword

A Brand-New Frame:
My Hopes for You

As I'm putting the finishing touches on *Picture Perfect,* the world has recently received some good body-image news— news that could help millions of girls feel more beautiful. Fashion Week 2006 made the front-page news in major newspapers around the world.

Fashion Week is an event where designers show their new collections for the upcoming year. It is held in different cities around the world. And Madrid, Spain, had the best Fashion Week ever!

In September 2006, Madrid's Fashion Week directors were concerned about the effects that skinny models have on girls' body image. They determined that skinny models are one reason so many millions of girls across the globe suffer from eating disorders and body-image problems. They told the models that they had to be a healthy weight, or they couldn't participate in Spain's Fashion Week. They couldn't be underweight, or they'd be sent home.

And it happened! Thirty percent of the models *were actually sent home* because they didn't weigh enough.

The message was clear: Models can be thin—as they have been for many decades—but they can't portray an image of emaciation and illness. They can be naturally thin, but they must be healthy!

Madrid's decision has made the whole world consider the negative effect that unhealthily skinny models have on a girl's and young woman's burgeoning body image and self-esteem. Other countries are talking about whether or not they'll support a ban on bone-thin models. This important debate within the fashion industry gives me hope that someday girls and women will no longer be barraged by a narrow, unhealthy definition of beauty.

To paraphrase the late John Lennon of the Beatles:

Imagine a world where girls and women don't feel like they need to be different from how they are to feel—and to be considered—beautiful.

Imagine a naturally thin girl who feels beautiful.

Imagine a naturally large girl who feels beautiful.

And imagine that if she's naturally somewhere in

between, as most girls are, she feels beautiful, too.

I hope this enlightened and sensitive act on the part of the Madrid directors takes hold in every other country's Fashion Week, including the United States of America. I hope that the world's designers gain the courage to use healthy models— and models of all different colors and ethnicities.

These are big, global hopes—and just think of the possibilities! If they become a reality, it's a win-win situation for everyone: the designers, because they'll show integrity by giving the girls and women who support them the important message that *you can be too thin*; the models, because they'll be healthy; and the entire human race, because all of us—female and male—will see that healthy, diverse images of women are things of beauty!

And here are my special hopes for you:

❶ I hope that when you feel bad about your body the girls' stories in *Picture Perfect* will help you feel better and less lonely.

❷ I hope the stories in *Picture Perfect* give you the inspiration you need to take good care of yourself and see yourself in a new frame as a vibrant, valuable, and beautiful girl.

③ I hope *Picture Perfect* will help fill your mind with Special Statements, or positive messages, about your body and yourself, and help you delete the garbage, or negative messages, you get from many TV shows, movies, and magazines.

④ I hope *Picture Perfect* will help inspire you and your friends to share your feelings about body image and support one another.

⑤ I hope you'll always use lots of Special Statements to picture yourself as *perfect*—forever!

Resources

Here's a list of websites, organizations, products, recipes, books, and CDs that the girls in *Picture Perfect* have put together for you.

When You Don't See the Beauty in You

Cari:

Cari thinks Ahava products are the best. "I learned about Ahava when I got my manicure and pedicure. I use the hand cream and foot cream. It's a little expensive, but it lasts a long time, and I think it's worth it. My hands were really chapped, and the hand cream worked really well." Ahava is made in Israel, but it's available in department stores and drugstores, or at www.ahavaus.com. Or try www.Dead-Sea-Beauty.com (click on "ahava," then "body care") for the hand cream and foot cream at discounted prices.

Julie:

Julie goes to an eating disorders support group. If you're interested in joining one, too, check out these sites for groups in your area, plus lots more information:

www.anad.org: (website for Anorexia Nervosa and Associated Disorders) a self-help resource for girls with eating disorders and their families. Also gives referrals for therapists who specialize in eating disorders.

www.oa.org: (website for Overeaters Anonymous) groups use the "12-step" approach to eating disorders.

Annie:

Annie gives you this recipe for a facial you can give yourself at home. Her doctor said it won't get rid of her acne, but it does make her skin feel silky and smooth. (If you have active acne, ask your doctor before you try this.)

Annie's At-Home Facial:

Take ½ cup oatmeal. Put in a blender. Blend for a few seconds, until it's a fine powder. Store in a plastic container.

Cleanse your face (with a gentle cleanser like Dove soap or Cetaphil) and rinse well. While your skin's still wet, put about a tablespoon of oatmeal powder in your wet hands, then gently massage for a few seconds on your wet face.

Rinse with warm (but not hot) water. Gently pat your face dry, and put on a little oil-free moisturizer if you like. Your face will feel soft, and the oatmeal exfoliates—it helps get rid of dead skin cells.

When Worries About Food and Weight Kidnap Your Life

Jess:

www.thebodypositive.org: Jess likes this website because it inspires her to calm down and feel better about her body. The "who we are" link has lots of good information, including how to start a body-image support peer group at your school. Jess says, "It's like a cyber comfort box. Click on the 'alterations art project.' It is especially cool."

Brandi:

Here are two books, both written by women soccer stars, that help Brandi feel good about being strong and athletic:

It's Not About the Bra: Play Hard, Play Fair, and Put the Fun Back into Competitive Sports, by Brandi Chastain (Collins, Reprint Ed., 2005).

Go for the Goal, by Mia Hamm (Harper, 2000).

Lindy:

Lindy loves the Beatles—she found her Special Statement, *Get back to where you once belonged,* in the song, "Get Back." These are her favorite Beatles CDs:

Love, The Beatles

The Beatles Greatest Hits

The Beatles, 1967–1970

When School's a Big Fashion Show

Suzy:

These two websites offer great discounts on clothes, accessories, and more!

www.target.com

www.daisymaze.com

Suzy says, "And don't forget resale shops, the Salvation Army stores, and H&M." (H&M is a British company with dozens of stores in the United States. To find a store in your area, go to www.hm.com.)

Alison:

Sewing 101: A Beginner's Guide to Sewing (Creative Publishing International, 2002).

Alison says, "This is a good book if you want to learn how to sew and can't find anyone to teach you."

Emily:

www.smartgirl.org: "This is a cool website. I just like it a lot. It has lots of things on it about body image and other stuff. It has creative things, like poems and art by girls. I'm thinking of writing a poem about having my own special style, and I hope they post it."

Dealing with Your Body Type

Alicia:

www.girlsinc.org: Alicia likes the "Just for Girls" link on this site. She says, "This website is empowering. It's got lots of surveys and quizzes and puzzles and fun stuff. Most of all, it helps me take my mind off my body-image problems."

Jenny:

Style Trix for Cool Chix, by Leanne Warrick (Watson-Guptill, 2005).

"I like this book, especially the 'Be Unique' chapter." This book has quizzes and gives advice on how to make the most of your body type, no matter what your shape.

Emma:

www.womenssportsfoundation.org: "I found this site by accident. But I like it a lot." You can click on the "Sports & Fitness" link, then click on "GoGirlGo" for information on sports stars and more, including a sports personality quiz to help you find the perfect sport for you.

Dealing with Perfectionism

Maggie:

www.campaignforrealbeauty.com: (the Dove Company's website). Maggie really likes this website because it helps keep her on a positive body-image track. Click on "inside the campaign" to find facts and information on body image—and to send your best friend a "real beauty" e-card!

Melly:

What Do You Know? Wisdom for the Road Ahead, edited by Jeanette Spires (Riverwood Books, 2005).

Melly says, "I like this book because it gives me some perspective on my problems. It has stories by lots of successful people about how they felt when they were growing up. It helps me stay rational when I get stressed out about how I look."

Tanya:

Um, Like . . . OM: A Girl Goddess's Guide to Yoga, by Evan Cooper (Little Brown & Co., 2005).

Tanya's aunt bought her this book for her birthday, and she loves it—it even includes yoga poses for positive body image!

Kick Boxing Basics, by Joe Fox and Art Michaels (Sterling Books, 1998).

Tanya says, "This is a book that my kickboxing teacher recommends. But I also recommend a class."

When You're Teased About Your Body

Elly:

www.geocities.com/angel.strength: Visit this website for information on the "I Am Beautiful, No Matter What They

Say" T-shirts. You can also order the shirts by e-mail at angel.strength@yahoo.com.

Faith:

www.easingtheteasing.com: This site has good information about teasing and bullying, including a poem and a reading list (both written by a girl who was teased). Faith's antibullying support group likes this site.

Angelina:

Here's a list of Angelina's favorite musicals. She says, "I love singing to these tunes!" You can check out the CDs at www.amazon.com.

Wicked

Hair

South Pacific

The King and I

Oklahoma!

Carousel

Dreamgirls (the 2006 film soundtrack features Jennifer Hudson and Beyonce Knowles)

West Side Story

The Sound of Music

High School Musical

When You're Honestly Overweight

Jesse:

Strong Women Stay Young, by Dr. Miriam E. Nelson (Bantam Books, 1997).

Not just for your mom—Jesse thinks this is a great fitness book. It has simple exercises, many using inexpensive free weights, to keep you toned and fit.

Denise:

Here's Denise's recipe for her favorite after-school snack. Her nutritionist helped her create it. Denise says, "You can buy hummus at the grocery store, but it's more fun to make it. I like a lot of garlic, but feel free to season to your own taste buds!"

Denise's Hummus:

1 can garbanzo beans

1 large garlic clove, minced

1 tbsp lemon juice

a little cayenne pepper

a little black pepper

$1/2$ tsp salt

5 tbsp tahini (sesame paste, available at the grocery store)

Put garbanzo beans, garlic, lemon juice, cayenne, black pepper, and salt in a blender or food processor. Blend until smooth. Add tahini. Blend about a minute. Eat with veggies like baby carrots or celery, or whole grain crackers.

Denise's nutritionist also recommended this book, which she's passing on to you. If you're seriously overweight, you may find it helpful too:

The Diet for Teenagers Only, by Carrie Wiatt (Regan Books, 2005).

Stacie:

Dealing with the Stuff That Makes Life Tough: The Ten Things That Stress Girls Out and How to Cope with Them, by Jill Zimmerman Rutledge, LCSW (Contemporary/McGraw-Hill, 2004).

Stacie says, "This book has lots of ways to cope with feelings."

The Alchemist, by Paulo Coelho (Harper/San Francisco, 1993).

Stacie says, "I like this book because it's spiritual, and it helps me feel better about myself. It makes me think of my life as a journey, and I like that idea."

Some Inspirations for Your Own Special Statement

Here are some quotations that may inspire you to feel better about your body, mind, and spirit. Quotes can come from the sayings of famous people, proverbs, poems, song lyrics, television interviews, overheard conversations—the sources for quotes are practically limitless. So keep your ears and eyes open. Add to the list. Quotes can give you some ideas to help you create your own unique, personal Special Statement.

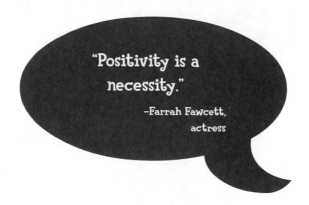

"Positivity is a necessity."

–Farrah Fawcett, actress

"If you compare yourself
with others, you may become
vain and bitter. For always there will be
greater and lesser persons than yourself.
Enjoy your achievements as
well as your plans."
–Anonymous

"I finally realized that being
grateful to my body was key to
giving more love to myself."
–Oprah Winfrey, talk-show host

"Worry is a misuse of
the imagination."
–Dan Zadra, author

"A beautiful thing is
never perfect."
–Egyptian proverb

"Problems are to the mind what exercise is to the muscles; they toughen and make strong."

–Norman Vincent Peale, motivational speaker, author

"People can alter their lives by altering their attitudes."

–William James, philosopher

"You are unique, and if that is not fulfilled, then something has been lost."

–Martha Graham, dancer

"Nobody can be you as effectively as you can."

–Norman Vincent Peale, motivational speaker, author

"The body is a sacred garment."

–Martha Graham, dancer

"The best cosmetic in the world is an active mind that is always finding something new."

–Mary Meek Atkeson, author

"You can't be brave if you've only had wonderful things happen to you."

–Mary Tyler Moore, actress

"Aware of my body, I breathe in. Smiling to my body, I breathe out."

–Thich Nhat Hanh, Buddhist monk

"Beauty is not about people telling you to look sexy. It's the confidence to be beautiful in your own way."

–Erykah Badu, singer/songwriter

"You must do the thing
you think you cannot do."

–Eleanor Roosevelt,
U.S. diplomat, social reformer

"Habits aren't broken as
much as replaced. It takes 25–30
repetitions to create
a new habit."

–Patricia Wells, author, chef

"Whatever my weight is,
that's fine. As long as I am able
to move and feel good,
it doesn't matter."

–Monica Seles, tennis pro

"(She) who sings
frightens away (her) ills."

–Spanish proverb

"People often say that
'beauty is in the eye of the beholder,'
and I say that the most liberating thing
about beauty is realizing that you are the
beholder. This empowers us to find beauty in
places where others have not dared to
look, including inside ourselves."

–Salma Hayek, actress

"Everything
has its beauty but not
everyone sees it."

–Confucious,
Chinese philosopher

"Be not ashamed of
mistakes and thus make
them crimes."

–Confucious, Chinese philosopher

"Our bodies are
our gardens."

–Shakespeare, playwright

"Hide not your talents,
for use they were made; what's
a sun-dial in the shade?"
—Ben Franklin,
author, inventor, diplomat

"A diamond with
a flaw is preferable to a
common stone with none."
—Chinese proverb

"Exuberance is
beauty."
—William Blake, poet

"The best part of
beauty is that which no
picture can express."
—Sir Francis Bacon,
British author, philosopher

"Size 12 is not fat."
—Meg Cabot, author

"Be gentle on yourself.
It's important to be gentle
and forgiving."
—Sheryl Crow, singer/songwriter

"Think of all the
beauty still left around
you and be happy."
—Anne Frank, diarist

"We are what
we repeatedly do."
—Aristotle,
Greek philosopher

"Don't waste yourself
in rejection, nor bark against
the bad, but chant the
beauty of the good."
—Ralph Waldo Emerson, poet

"Never bend your head. Hold it high, look the world straight in the eye."

–Helen Keller, educator, author

"The absence of flaw in beauty is itself a flaw."

–Havelock Ellis, British psychologist

"I stand in awe of my body."

–Henry David Thoreau, author, philosopher

"A journey of 1,000 miles begins with a single step."

–Lao-tzu, Chinese philosopher

"If anything
is sacred the human
body is sacred."

–Walt Whitman, poet

"Be not
fearful of happiness."

–Lao-tzu,
Chinese philosopher

"Each individual
woman's body demands to
be accepted on its
own terms."

–Gloria Steinem,
author, feminist

Index

A

acceptance
  body, 7–8
  body types and, 80
acne, 18–21
Action Plans
  Alicia's story and, 85
  Alison's story and, 66
  Angelina's story and, 143–45
  Annie's story and, 21
  Brandi's story and, 89
  Cari's story and, 11–12
  Denise's story and, 171–75
  Elly's story and, 133–35
  Emily's story and, 70–71
  Emma's story and, 94–95
  Faith's story and, 138–39
  Jenny's story and, 88–90
  Jesse's story and, 161–66
  Jess's story and, 34–36
  Julie's story and, 16–17
  Lindy's story and, 44–45
  Maggie's story and, 108–10
  Melly's story and, 114–17
  Stacie's story and, 179–83
  Suzy's story and, 58–62
  Tanya's story and, 121
Alicia's story, 81–85
Alison's story, 62–66
alterations, fashion and, 70–71
ANAD, vii
Angelina's story, 140–45
Annie's story, 18–21
anorexia. *See* eating disorders
Anorexia Nervosa and Associated
  Disorders (ANAD). *See* ANAD
anxiety
  body image and, 6–7
  perfectionism and, 103

B

bat mitzvahs, 157
baths, bubble, 195

behaviors, replacing, 181–83
"Beyond Stereotypes: Rebuilding the
  Foundation of Beauty Belief", 190
bloating, x, 153
blood pressure, high, 168
BMI, 154
body acceptance, 7–8
body image
  Annie's story and, 18–21
  body types and, 79
  Cari's story and, 8–12
  complexity of, 189–90
  distortions of, 3–4
  Julie's story and, 13–17
  pampering and, 195–96
  perfectionism and, 103 (*see also*
    perfectionism)
  positive feelings about, 7–8
  quiz, 4
  reasons for distortions of, 5–6
  Special Statements for, 8, 13
  teasing and, 147
  working toward improving, 22–24
body image Distortion Quiz, 4
Body Mass Index, 154
body types
  Alicia's story and, 81–85
  Emma's story and, 91–95
  fashion and, 67
  Jenny's story and, 86–90
  learning to appreciate, 95–98
  understanding, 77–81
Brandi's story, 36–39
breast reduction surgery, 87
bubble baths, 195
budgeting, 58–59
bulimia. *See* eating disorders
bullies, teasing and, 128–29.
  See also teasing
Burbank, Luther, 101

C

calming chair, 117

carbs. *See* food
cardiovascular disease, 168
Cari's story, 8–12
Centers for Disease Control, 156
Chang, Sarah, 101
changes, gradual, 8
cholesterol, 168
comebacks, body types and, 89–90
comfort, food as, 176–77
comfort boxes, 35–36
comparisons, with others, 5
conceit, body image and, 5
control, body types and, 80
counseling
  depression and, 176, 184–85
  eating disorders and, 41–43,
    112–13, 114–15
  nutritional, 169–70
  teasing and, 147
creativity
  Alison's story and, 62–66
  special statements and, 47
culture
  message to girls and, xi
  preoccupation with food and
    weight and, 28
curves, maturity and, 7

D
Denise's story, 166–75
depression
  body image and, 6–7
  perfectionism and, 103
  Stacie's story and, 175–83
dessert. *See* food
diabetes, 168
dieting, 79. *See also* food
diversity, body types and, 78
divorce, Alison's story and, 62–63
Dove, 190

E
eating disorders
  Julie's story and, 13–17
  Lindy's story and, 41
  Melly's story and, 110–17

  perfectionism and, 103
  suspicion of, ix
  thinness vs., 133–34
elegance, fashion and, 67–71
Elly's story, 130–35
Emily's story, 67–71
Emma's story, 91–95
emotions
  developing positive, 47–48
  eating disorders and, 13, 15
  reframing, xiii–xiv
  replacement behaviors and,
    181–83
  Stacie's story and, 179–80
  true, 24
empowerment, perfectionism and, 123
exercise
  Denise's story and, 173–75
  healthy amounts of, 80, 98
  importance of, 193
  Jesse's story and, 160, 161
  Julie's story and, 16–17

F
Faith's story, 135–39
family
  as mirrors, 3
  trust and, ix
fashion
  Alison's story and, 62–66
  body types and, 88–89, 93–94, 98
  confusion about, 53–54
  Emily's story and, 67–71
  Fashion Week and, 197–99
  new ways of looking at, 71–73
  pressure and, 51–54
  Suzy's story and, 55–62
Fashion Week, 197–99
fast foods, 160
fat
  eating disorders and (*see* eating
    disorders)
  as an emotion, 13
  importance of, 155
  overweight and (*see* overweight)
  types of, 170–71
feelings. *See* emotions

flaws, 24
food
    Brandi's story and, 36–39
    comfort and, 176–77
    finding a balance with, 45–48
    healthy eating and, 80, 98, 155–56,
        160, 162–66, 171–73
    Jess's story and, 31–36
    Lindy's story and, 40–45
    Melly's story and, 110–17
    metabolism and, 79
    preoccupation with, 28–30
    quiz, 27
    school lunches and, 162–63
A Food and Weight Quiz, 27
foot massages, 195
Freedman, Lynn, 155
fried foods, 160
friends
    importance of, 194
    as mirrors, 3
    sharing experiences with, 34–35
    spending and, 61
    teasing and, 147, 149
    trust and, ix
fun, preoccupation with weight and,
    28, 37

G
girls, teasing and, 127
gradual changes, 8
guilt, body image and, 5

H
habits, body image and, 5
happiness, fashion and, 57
HDL, 168
high blood pressure, 168
hormones, body types and, 92–93
hypertension, 168

I
illogical thoughts, body image and, 6
imperfections, as unique characteris-
    tics, 24
information, learning new, 183–84

insecurity
    body image and, 5–6, 9
    teasing and, 130
inspiration, for teens, 199–200
integrity, 148–49
irrational thoughts
    body image and, 6
    Melly's story and, 110–17

J
jealousy, body image and, 8
Jenny's story, 86–90
Jesse's story, 157–66
Jess's story, 31–36
jogging. *See* exercise
Julie's story, 13–17

K
kickboxing, 121. *See also* exercise
King, Martin Luther, Jr., 101
knowledge, importance of, 44–45

L
LDL, 168
lunch, school, 162–63

M
Maggie's story, 106–10
mantras. *See* Special Statements
maturity
    anxiety and, 7
    early, 118
medication
    acne and, 18–19
    trichotillomania and, 141
Melly's story, 110–17
menstruation
    bloating and, x, 153
    hormones and, 93
metabolism, 78–79
mirrors, friends and family as, 3
modesty, body image and, 5
money, teen spending and, 52

N
name-calling, 128
National Crime Prevention Council, 127
negativity, perfectionism and, 102–4
nutritional counseling, 169–70

O
obesity, 156. *See also* overweight
overweight
    coming to terms with, 153–57
    dealing with in a healthy way,
      183–85
    Denise's story and, 166–75
    Jesse's story and, 157–66
    Stacie's story and, 175–83

P
pampering, 195–96
pedicures, 195
peers. *See* friends
perfection, expectations of, xi. *See*
  also perfectionism
perfectionism
    defined, 101
    focusing positively, 122–23
    looks and, ix
    Maggie's story and, 106–10
    Melly's story and, 110–17
    quiz, 102, 103
    Tanya's story and, 118–21
    understanding, 101–5
periods. *See* menstruation
pimples. *See* acne
positive self-thoughts. *See also*
  Special Statements
    Annie's story and, 20
    body types and, 98
    development of, 47–48
    fashion and, 68–69
    importance of, 7–8
    perfectionism and, 105
puberty. *See* maturity

Q
qualities, my unique, 24
quizzes

body image distortions and, 4
food and weight and, 27
perfectionism and, 102, 104

R
reframing, thoughts and feelings,
  xiii–xiv
relaxation, importance of, 193–94
resilience, 140–42, 146
role models, 148–49

S
sales, shopping and, 59–62
satisfaction with looks, ix–x
savings. *See* budgeting
school
    fashion and (*see* fashion)
    lunches and, 162–63
    support groups and, 194
    teasing and, 128–29
    uniforms and, 63
self-esteem
    perfectionism and, 103
    preoccupation with weight and, 28
    Special Statements and, 192
    teasing and, 147, 149
sewing, fashion and, 65, 70–71
shapes. *See* body types
shopping
    fashion and (*see* fashion)
    smart, 59–62
    teens and, 52–53 (*see also* fashion)
singing, as Action Plan, 144–45
sleep, importance of, 193–94
soups, as healthy food choice, 164–66
Special Statements
    Alicia's story and, 81
    Alison's story and, 62
    Angelina's story and, 140
    Annie's story and, 18
    brainstorming, 148–49
    Brandi's story and, 36
    Cari's story and, 8
    Denise's story and, 166
    design of, 24
    Elly's story and, 130

Emily's story and, 67
Emma's story and, 91
Faith's story and, 135
importance of, 192–93
introduction to, xi–xiii
Jenny's story and, 86
Jesse's story and, 157
Jess's story and, 31
Julie's story and, 13
Lindy's story and, 40
Maggie's story and, 106
Melly's story and, 110
Stacie's story and, 175
Suzy's story and, 55
Tanya's story and, 118
spending
    fashion and (*see* fashion)
    teens and, 52
Stacie's story, 175–83
support groups
    eating disorders and, 14–15
    schools and, 194
    teasing and, 147, 149
surgery, breast reduction, 87
Suzy's story, 55–62
sweets. *See* food

T
Tanya's story, 118–21
teasing
    Angelina's story and, 140–45
    dealing with, 127–30
    Elly's story and, 130–35
    Faith's story and, 135–39

getting past, 145–49
prevalence of, 127
weight and, ix
thoughts
    developing positive, 47–48
    illogical/irrational, 6
    reframing, xiii–xiv
thrift shopping, 59–62
trichotillomania, 140
trust, body types and, 98

U
uniforms, school, 63

W
walking, 161. *See also* exercise
weight
    Brandi's story and, 36–39
    finding a balance with, 45–48
    Jess's story and, 31–36
    Lindy's story and, 40–45
    overweight and (*see* overweight)
    preoccupation with, 28–30
    quiz, 27
weight loss, healthy, 159–66
Wicked, 144
The Wizard of Oz, xi–xii, 191
Woods, Tiger, 101

Z
zits. *See* acne